D0048089

A CHINA BUSINESS PRIMER

The COVID-19 pandemic underscored longstanding fissures in China's business relationships with the West. If the West is going to develop a relationship of mutual trust and improve business relations with China in the coming decades, it is imperative to understand how to engage with Chinese thinking on ethics in business—this book explains how.

Government officials, businesspeople, and business-ethicists have trouble communicating about issues in ethics, policy, and business across the China-West divide. This book shows how to overcome the us-versus-them mindset plaguing China-West relations by presenting to Western audiences an easy-to-understand yet deeply informed primer on core ideas and perspectives in Chinese cultural and philosophical thought. The book considers original texts of Chinese philosophy and religion, and applies principles from those writings to three business-ethics topics of enduring interest to business executives, government officials, and academics, namely, the protection of intellectual property, assurance of product safety and quality in the pharmaceutical supply chain, and human rights.

This book is a must-read for those who want to forge constructive relationships with their Chinese counterparts based on mutual trust and understanding. The book is specifically relevant to business executives, but it should also be of interest to policymakers, educators, and students who seek to communicate more effectively with their Chinese counterparts, in particular about difficult and contentious business, policy, and ethical issues.

Michael A. Santoro is the author of two previous books about China. A former Fulbright Fellow at the University of Hong Kong, he has taught at the Sinopec Management Institute and Shanghai Jiao Tong University. He is a professor of management and entrepreneurship at Santa Clara University.

Robert Shanklin is Senior Lecturer in the Philosophy Department at Santa Clara University. His teaching and publications include Chinese philosophy, business ethics, aesthetics, and philosophy of language. He has advised firms based in Silicon Valley and elsewhere on business ethics and China.

"Well-researched, lucidly written, and bristling with insights, *A China Business Primer* offers a clear and effective practical guide to help contemporary Westerners navigate the uncharted waters of ethical practices, norms, and expectations in the Chinese business world."

—Philip J. Ivanhoe, Chair of the Department of East Asian Languages and Cultures,
Georgetown University, USA

"All of us who engage with contemporary China—in business, academia, and NGOs—encounter a world of references deeply held by our Chinese counterparts. This book arms you with those cultural/historical touchstones, and illuminates the Chinese approach to ethics (and how it differs from Western thinking). Up to date and essential knowledge for building your credibility and ethical fluency in today's China."

—David Youtz, President, Yale-China Association, USA

A CHINA BUSINESS PRIMER

Ethics, Culture, and Relationships

Michael A. Santoro
and
Robert Shanklin

Routledge
Taylor & Francis Group

LONDON AND NEW YORK

First published 2021
by Routledge
2 Park Square, Milton Park, Abingdon, Oxon OX14 4RN

and by Routledge
52 Vanderbilt Avenue, New York, NY 10017

Routledge is an imprint of the Taylor & Francis Group, an informa business

British Library Cataloguing-in-Publication Data
A catalogue record for this book is available from the British Library

Library of Congress Cataloging-in-Publication Data
Names: Santoro, Michael A., author. | Shanklin, Robert, 1980– author.
Title: A China business primer : ethics, culture, and relationships / Michael A.
  Santoro and Robert Shanklin.
Description: Abingdon, Oxon ; New York, NY : Routledge, 2021. | Includes
  bibliographical references and index.
Identifiers: LCCN 2020040513 (print) | LCCN 2020040514 (ebook) |
  ISBN 9780367506698 (hbk) | ISBN 9780367506711 (pbk) |
  ISBN 9781003050711 (ebk)
Subjects: LCSH: Business ethics—China. | Human rights—China. |
  Intellectual property—China. | Product safety—China.
Classification: LCC HF5387.5.C6 S35 2021 (print) | LCC HF5387.5.C6 (ebook) |
  DDC 174/.40951—dc23
LC record available at https://lccn.loc.gov/2020040513
LC ebook record available at https://lccn.loc.gov/2020040514

ISBN: 978-0-367-50669-8 (hbk)
ISBN: 978-0-367-50671-1 (pbk)
ISBN: 978-1-003-05071-1 (ebk)

Typeset in Joanna
by Apex CoVantage, LLC

To Robyn Burch

MAS

* * *

To the late Jim Higginbotham, dissertation supervisor, steadfast supporter and friend who, while correcting my Chinese, encouraged me to continue my studies of Chinese language, culture and philosophy, even as I delved into the realms of formal syntax and semantics. Jim, I'm sorry you never got to see my first publication, and I wish you had gotten to see this book.

RS

CONTENTS

FIGURES

ACKNOWLEDGMENTS

We want to thank our editor at Routledge Press, Rebecca Marsh. Rebecca supported our project with inspiring enthusiasm and had the publisher's vision to see where our initial proposal might head and how to get there.

We are grateful to a number of friends and colleagues who have generously read and commented on drafts of the book. We especially want to thank the following: Meilin Chinn, P. J. Ivanhoe, Howard Barnet, Haoning Richter, and Larry Bridwell.

We are also grateful to Gigi Etem and Brennan Lagerstrom for their excellent work helping us prepare the manuscript, especially for their skillful mastery of the citations and references.

* * *

Michael A. Santoro wishes to make the following acknowledgments: I have been traveling to China for nearly three decades, teaching, visiting factories, and discussing the issues in this book with Chinese and Western managers and government officials, as well as advocates who work in NGOs. Although they cannot all be named and most would prefer not to be, I want to express my appreciation to them for helping me to learn about the real-world opportunities and challenges of doing business in China.

I am also very grateful to my many friends and colleagues in the Society for Business Ethics, the Global Business and Human Rights Scholars

Association, and the Teaching Forum on Business and Human Rights. I feel truly blessed and honored to know such brilliant scholars, teachers, and advocates for justice. Their collective knowledge and wisdom, generously shared, constitute an important foundation for this book. I say this even with the expectation that many of them are at the ready to voice skepticism of what they read herein.

Last, but decidedly not least, I want to thank my wife, Robyn Burch, to whom I dedicate this book. As hard as I worked to complete it, she worked that much harder to maintain some semblance of order in our home for us and our children, Jack and Guy. This book was completed while sheltering in place during the COVID-19 pandemic and so, as many families can attest, that made the burdens on us even greater. Robyn's unbounded love, humor, grace, and pure grit got us through it and made it all worthwhile. Our sons, Jack and Guy, are too young to read this, but when they are old enough to do so, I want them to know that they bring unbounded joy and wonderment into our lives. I love you more than the moon!

* * *

Robert Shanklin wishes to make the following personal acknowledgments: I owe a great debt of gratitude to Bryan W. Van Norden, who started me on the path that led here during my freshman year of college. Since then he has been a guide and inspiration on matters personal as well as professional, exemplifying the principles, values, and ideals we promote in this book. This debt is the sort that can be repaid only by paying it forward to future scholars whom I encounter early in their careers.

Another immense debt of gratitude I owe to my parents, Bob and Jan, and my sister Jen—for everything—but in particular for our "1pm pact" during our visits, which allowed me much-needed time to work on this book every morning and early afternoon.

A special thank-you goes to thank Meilin Chinn, my co-conspirator and the co-organizer of the 2018 Fagothey Philosophy Conference, *Value: East and West*. Meilin's generosity of spirit, together with her pervading Daoist calm, help make the world a more harmonious place. The participants and attendees of that conference—P. J. Ivanhoe, David Wong, Vrinda Dalmiya, Leah Kalmanson, Justin Tiwald, as well as many students and faculty of Santa Clara—provided an unfathomable wealth of valuable perspectives and expertise on Asian cultures and philosophies.

I am deeply appreciative of my colleagues in the Santa Clara University Philosophy Department, especially Philip Kain, Christopher Kulp, and Michael Meyer, who provided constant encouragement during the writing of this book, as well as much-needed personal support as I faced health-related challenges along the way.

Finally, I am profoundly grateful to John Ahern, who was one of the first to show me the way through the sometimes savage, rugged, and fierce forest of academic scholarship, and who showed me how to persevere even when the clear path ahead is obscured.

1

TEA WITH THE DRAGON

Traditional Chinese ethics and contemporary Chinese business

The need for business executives and government officials to understand and communicate with their Chinese counterparts has become a matter of great urgency. Whether you believe China and the West are "destined for war," allies, or "strategic competitors," whether you believe the 21st century belongs to China or you think China is heading toward cataclysmic economic and social collapse, whether you believe new social media platforms like WeChat undermine the Communist Party's grip over civil society or you think the government will use new technologies such as facial recognition to tighten authoritarian control, whether you are a human rights advocate or a business executive eager to do deals, whether you think China exacerbated the global death toll of COVID-19 by suppressing information about the virus or you believe it was the victim of xenophobia and racism, the need for mutual understanding and effective intercultural communication has never been greater.

The year 2020 marked perhaps the most perilous and contentious moment between China and the West since the 1989 Tiananmen Square massacre. China's crackdown on democratic protests in Hong Kong raised global human rights concerns. News headlines offer a daily drumbeat of saber rattling, trade sanctions, and retaliations. Some of China's most important global technology companies like Huawei and TikTok have prompted security concerns among a number of Western nations. Because of these rising tensions and the impact of the COVID-19 virus, the number of Chinese students studying in the West has plummeted and so has travel by Westerners to China for business, education, and tourism. In many respects, this book, emphasizing as it does the importance of understanding traditional Chinese culture, would seem to be coming out at the worst time, when China and the West are at loggerheads. While we are mindful that the conflicts between China and the West are real and unlikely to dissipate anytime soon, we are nonetheless hopeful that if Westerners absorb the ideas and lessons of this book, they will be in a much better position to manage those conflicts in a manner that will minimize the potential for human suffering and economic destruction on both sides, and perhaps even help illuminate a path to areas of common interests.

This book elucidates some central ideas in the most essential writings of traditional Chinese culture with the purpose of helping Westerners to communicate more effectively with their Chinese counterparts, in particular about difficult and contentious business ethics issues. It is specifically addressed to business executives, but it should also be of interest to government officials, educators, and students. It is a book about the continuing relevance of traditional approaches to ethics in contemporary China. We use the term "traditional" not as a euphemism for "pre-modern," "primitive," or simply "old," but rather to highlight traditions in thought and behavior that have been, and continue to be, enduring aspects of everyday thinking, behavior, and culture. We draw on classics of literature and philosophy written and transmitted steadfastly over the course of millennia. By focusing on the most essential ideas in traditional Chinese culture, we open a window for Westerners who want to understand Chinese approaches to ethical thinking and decision-making, and how they affect business behavior and other interactions with foreigners. We apply the principles set forth in the book to three business ethics topics of enduring interest to business executives, government officials, and academics, namely, the protection of intellectual property, assurance of product safety and quality in the pharmaceutical supply chain, and human rights.

A central theme of this book is that engaging with Chinese perspectives on ethical thought and behavior does not amount to a relativistic "going native" or, as the old adage goes, "when in Rome, do as the Romans do." To the contrary, as we shall demonstrate, familiarity with the basic tenets of traditional Chinese culture is an essential component of effective advocacy for bedrock ethical, human rights, public policy, as well as business principles and interests.

As frustrating and unjust as it may be for human rights advocates and business ethicists to accept, the plain fact is that traditional Chinese culture does not emphasize the welcoming of foreign cultural perspectives, freedom of expression, being a cultural melting pot, resisting religious persecution, or correcting political injustice. For millennia, China has functioned through centralized authoritarian bureaucracy controlling the populace, politics, and the economy. Entry-level notions in Western approaches to ethics—such as equality, liberty, property rights, human rights, and maximizing happiness—are just that. They are not entry-level notions in Chinese approaches to ethics. This is crucial for understanding why, as many managers of Western multinational companies report from working in China, demands and justifications for ethical behavior that make sense to Westerners seem to fall on deaf ears in China.

What counts as ethics in the first place, and hence what counts as a justification for why some decision or act is ethical or not, are not even recognizably the same in many cases (Roetz, 2009). To take a general example, the claim that some act would be wrong because it does not treat others equally would be unrecognizable as a justification for ethical wrongness in a Chinese cultural-philosophical context. Whereas Western perspectives on what is just often hinge on notions of what is fair and equitable, Chinese perspectives on what is just hinge on the particular nature of the relationships between and among individuals and groups. Thus, from a Chinese perspective, what counts as just treatment of a business partner would depend, not on their status as a human being or on them (simply) being a partner, but on how long one has known them and how personal the relationship is.

Our motivation for writing about traditional Chinese culture is not to exalt cultural excuses to mistreat workers, take quality and safety shortcuts, or justify intellectual property theft. Rather, we believe it holds the key to achieving progress on these very contentious issues. It is a paradox to be sure, but one we embrace wholly. It is a fundamental premise of this book that to achieve progress on these bedrock Western and modern business

[handwritten margin notes:]

*control
1. populace
2. politics
3. economy*

What is ethical in one culture may not be in another culture. Ex: America/Western & China

relationships are what matter most... loyalty

not aiming to blame, or excuse behaviors, but to make progress in contentious issues practices and ethical precepts, one must learn to be agile with respect to traditional Chinese culture. Indeed, importance of developing a capacity for such cultural "agility" is one of the main takeaways of this book.

1.1 Beware of green hats: what you don't know about traditional Chinese culture can sink your prospects

Given the multiplicity of cultural forces at work in China today and the contestation and reinvention of the meaning of traditional values over the course of millennia, a book that seeks to gain insight from its most ancient philosophical writings in the contemporary business environment might seem hopelessly quixotic and out of touch. Moreover, especially among young people born and raised since the 1980s, social scientists have observed the development of bi-cultural and multicultural adaptations of traditional values in response to the forces of economic transformation (Hu et al., 2018). However, the very real discontinuities, contestability, and multiplicity of Chinese culture should not mask its extraordinary degree of continuity, coherence, and enduring relevance. Despite the many forces drawing contemporary China in divergent directions, its culture and traditions remain remarkably resilient and distinctive, and they persist to this day in the country's political, social, business, and family life. For all the things that have changed in the momentous past century, remaining remarkably consistent are the thought-traditions that underpin Chinese culture: the ones that make Chinese thinking and practice surrounding ethics and business Chinese. These are a combination of philosophical, religious, and what might be termed "superstitious" traditions, which are all crucially relevant for understanding everyday Chinese life, including in business.

When we invoke the concept of culture in relation to the enduring resonance of traditional Chinese values in contemporary business, we take our cue from the Dutch social psychologist Geert Hofstede, who observed:

> understanding people means understanding their background, from which present and future behavior can be predicted. Their background has provided them with a certain culture. The word "culture" is used here in the sense of "the collective programming of the mind which distinguishes the members of one category of people from another."
>
> (Hofstede, 1994)

In short, Hofstede observes that culture distinguishes who people are and how they will be likely to behave. Traditional religio-philosophical elements of Chinese culture, we argue, are important components of that collective programming at work in contemporary China.

One primary reason for the ongoing relevance of ancient thought traditions is well-rehearsed: China has over 3,000 years of history, but unlike other old cultures, China's is not merely old. China has grown old in situ—in pretty much the same place, with many of the same common cultural references. It has also had continuity (if evolutionarily so) in its language and writing system. As a result, there has been a great deal of continuity over the millennia, specifically of the things that often make a culture what it is, including language, philosophy, religion, and art. To make the contrast vivid, consider that China was first unified in 221 BCE. In the West, it would be as if most of Europe, the Middle East, and North Africa still viewed themselves as Roman subjects, spoke and wrote something that was recognizably Latin, and could directly trace myriad everyday elements of their culture, thought, and behavior back to Rome. Therefore, in order to understand how Chinese people in the 21st century think and act in general, and especially with regard to ethics, one has to understand not just the ideas and practices that are more recently influential—such as of guānxi (關係) and "face" (which translates two Chinese concepts miànzi, 面子 and liǎn 臉)—but also other subtly influential ancient and enduring ones. In the case of China in particular, this means going back to foundational values that have shaped Chinese culture, especially Chinese thought and behavior, to this day. We therefore focus more on the philosophical, religious, and ultimately cultural undergirding that drives Chinese ways of thinking about ethics.[1]

Understanding the title of this chapter, "Tea with the dragon," like many things to do with China, requires understanding multiple aspects of Chinese

---

1   In what follows, we will emphasize ideas from Confucian and Daoist (also spelled "Taoist") texts, as well as ideas that resist any particular classification and are sometimes called "popular religion" (Adler, 2002, pp. 17–18). While some scholars write of the "Three Teachings" (sān jiào, 三教) of Chinese culture: Confucianism, Daoism, and Buddhism, we do not emphasize Buddhism because in China, Buddhism has been influenced by indigenous thought-systems, especially Daoism (Adler, 2002, pp. 74–89). Moreover, our focus is on contemporary business practices in China, and, although ideas from Buddhism have some salience in business, core Buddhist ideas such as karma, rebirth, and impermanence have considerably more influence in other spheres of life, such as private life and education (Adler, 2002, pp. 121–123).

culture. Tea has been a popular daily beverage in China since the ninth century, and is a symbol of Chinese identity and culture (Sigley, 2015). Sitting down to tea with someone is an act of hospitality, serving a ritualistic purpose and creating a social bond (Benn, 2015). The dragon symbolizes China itself, as it is a legendary creature so strongly associated with Chinese mythology, folklore, and popular culture. It is a symbol of strength, power, and good fortune. Thus, sitting down to tea with the dragon metaphorically captures one aim we have for this book, something that is so desperately needed: for Chinese and Western business executives, government officials, and others to approach China-West relations as involving opportunities to be polite, sit down, and have real conversations, *especially* when they have deep and serious areas of disagreement. This is in contrast to the animosity, excessive saber rattling, and widespread misperceptions, even ignorance, of Chinese culture that permeates much of the current international political climate.

Throughout this book, we demonstrate through a number of carefully chosen case studies how understanding and being able to apply the core ideas of classical Chinese philosophy and literature can help executives to achieve their business objectives and maintain their core ethical values when doing business in China. To take this path with us, it is not necessary to understand Chinese language, although we will be introducing a few Chinese words into the vocabulary of most readers. We hope to "translate" difficult and often subtle cultural ideas and traditions for the modern business executive, policy maker, academic, or student. We focus on these cultural elements because they continue to resonate in the modern world, even if Westerners don't realize that these traditional ideas might be forming an unstated backdrop to their business interactions.

Brewer Stone, a private equity investor who has been traveling to China for over three decades, offers a vivid portrait of how things can go very wrong when foreign business executives are oblivious to cultural signals:

> The most common problem scenario I have seen would tend to go as follows: 1) high level meeting between the US and Chinese leaders of their respective business. A lot of mutual compliments, perhaps a bit of framing of high-level opportunities for collaboration, and maybe even a general understanding of a path forward (amidst friendly toasts). The US side leaves happy and discusses a compelling opportunity internally. Then 2) the Chinese side sends a mid-tier person to speak with

someone who seems culturally connected—a Chinese national or speaker on the US company's staff for example—and describes some key terms that matter or something not so great (e.g. a favor or more) that needs to happen to get someone on the Chinese side on board. 3) The US side takes this move from the polite high level to the tougher indirect channel as demonstrating a lack of good faith, double talk, or some other bad act. The discussions end up with a lot of noise and the opportunity has to be truly compelling to fight all the way through to a close.

(Stone, Interview, 2020)

As further evidence of the relevance of traditional culture in contemporary business, consider the infamous "Green Hat" story relayed by John Kamm, the founder and chairman of the Dui Hua Foundation, a human rights organization and nonprofit humanitarian organization that promotes universal human rights in "well-informed, mutually respectful dialogue with China." Kamm, a MacArthur "genius" award recipient, has served as past president of the American Chamber of Commerce in Hong Kong and managed business operations in China for Occidental Chemical Company in the 1980s. "An American agricultural company wanted to secure an agreement to conduct field tests for their pesticide on a Chinese state farm," Kamm recalls.

It brought boxes of hats emblazoned with the company's name, trademark, and trademark color which was green. It was unable to hand out the hats however because in Chinese "to wear a green hat" means your wife or girlfriend is cheating on you.

(Kamm, Interview, 2020)

1.2 Beyond the good manners your mom taught you

In the early years of Chinese reform, if you sat down to breakfast at a hotel in Guangzhou, Beijing, Shanghai, or Chengdu, it was common to overhear Western business people (often quite loudly) lecturing their Chinese counterparts about one or another aspect of "how business was done" or what life was like in the West. All the talking went in one direction as so many Chinese citizens were eager to learn about the ways of the free market and the West. Everyone was an expert. Walking down the street, it was common to be approached by a perfect stranger wanting only to practice their English. They were glorious years for the pioneers who arrived first in China. One of us vividly recalls a particularly lurid example of what we call "Westsplaining" at breakfast in a Shanghai hotel as a particularly exuberant US businessman described his extensive gun collection to a group of wide-eyed Chinese executives. Slowly but surely in the intervening decades that dynamic has shifted. Today, Westerners who want to engage effectively with China need to listen as much as they talk. A business school professor might as likely be treated to a lecture about Hayek as be asked a question about supply and demand.

Most Western travelers to China have a vague understanding of guānxi and "face." These are indeed crucial cultural touchstones. We devote a chapter to each of these concepts. However, as we shall demonstrate, they are poorly understood and mostly inappropriately put into action by foreigners. Four decades after China opened up to the West, the level of understanding of Chinese cultural and ethical norms among Western businesspeople remains dangerously rudimentary. The result is miscommunication and missed opportunities. While some areas of disagreement, such as human rights, may never be fully bridged, most areas of concern such as product safety and quality and intellectual property have a lot of room for improvement. And even progress on contentious subjects like human rights can be better accomplished with greater cultural understanding.

What accounts for the dearth of understanding among Westerners about Chinese culture and traditions? In part, it must be admitted that the subject is a difficult one. Chinese languages often prove very difficult for Westerners to master. The culture behind the language is even harder for many Westerners to grasp. While it is true that a foreigner might find it difficult to master the subtle nuances of the French language, society, and culture, Chinese culture and traditions are especially complex and nuanced in part because they date back for millennia rather than centuries.

Many foreign business leaders have diverse reasons and rationalizations for resisting a deep dive into understanding their Chinese counterparts. At a recent business conference of business executives discussing product safety and quality in their manufacturing operations, we shared our ambitions to write a book about the importance of understanding traditional Chinese culture to doing business in China and engaging with Chinese counterparts in regard to difficult topics, especially in business ethics. We were greeted with a host of objections. One executive alluded to the good manners his mom taught him. "I find that if I treat my Chinese counterparts with the respect my mom taught me," he said, "that is what I need to be understood and do business effectively." Another executive said that "plain talk" is what Chinese people understand and appreciate, and implied that he did not need additional training in cultural understanding. While we agree that good manners and plain speaking are virtues that will certainly translate with many Chinese counterparts, we were surprised to hear that these executives believed them to be substitutes for cultural understanding and sensitivity. One executive averred that cultural understanding was not that important because if Chinese businesses want to participate in global markets they would have to conform to the language and standards of international business. Again, there is a lot of truth to the view that uniform global standards form the linchpin of a globalized economy, but it does not make sense to us that this would be interposed as an excuse for eschewing attention to local culture and tradition. Both ideas, as the business ethicist Tom Donaldson has written, can be simultaneously true (Donaldson, 1996).

We don't expect (or encourage) business executives who read this book to put aside the good manners their parents taught them or their plain good sense. Such virtues are as much valued in China as they are in the West. Nor do we deny that participation in the global economy will (to some extent) compel Chinese business executives to adhere to international standards. What we ask is that the reader maintain an open mind about supplementing their Western ideas about effective communication and interaction with normative concepts and foundational values drawn from a deep reservoir of Chinese tradition and culture that are needed to understand fully what guides and motivates their Chinese counterparts.

1.3 The "China Century" revisited: a brief survey of recent Chinese history and its opening to the West

In this and the two subsequent sections we offer a very brief and highly selective survey of modern and contemporary Chinese history—from the national humiliations at the hands of foreign powers in the 19th century to the founding of the People's Republic of China in 1949, the beginning of the reform era roughly 30 years later, the Tiananmen Square massacre in

1989, and the post-COVID-19 world we now live in. We make no claim to writing a complete or authoritative history.[2] However, a fundamental premise of this book is that understanding history is particularly important to understanding China's present—more important, we contend, than it is to understanding contemporary Europe or the relatively fledgling United States. What follows is a primer for those unfamiliar with the arc of modern and contemporary Chinese history in the reform era. Readers with deep grounding in this history may wish to skip ahead to Sections 1.5 and 1.6 where we discuss the persistence of classical Chinese culture in, respectively, contemporary Chinese society and Chinese business.

Many have predicted the 21st century would be the "China Century," suggesting that China will economically, politically, and perhaps even militarily dominate the world. How can one assess such claims in the third decade of the century? Close examination demonstrates that some fears and predictions have come true while others need mid-course revision.

Before there was a China Century, there were Chinese Millennia. Over its long imperial history, China looked around and perceived that it was the largest, most populous, richest, most powerful, and most culturally sophisticated civilization on Earth. For thousands of years, it was simply a given that all surrounding cultures and civilizations were "barbarian." The infamous "Memorial on the Bone of Buddha" (written 1,200 years ago) illustrates how long-standing this attitude of cultural superiority has been. The author, Han Yu, was a Confucian scholar and imperial official who served four Tang Dynasty emperors. In the "Memorial" he criticized Buddhism as "a cult of the barbarian peoples" and argued against any show of official support for Buddhism in China. Han took it for granted that the Emperor would be receptive to this anti-foreign perspective, but he miscalculated. Emperor Xianzong instead ordered Han's execution, which was eventually commuted to exile (Wu-Chi, 1990, pp. 126–127). Han's presumption, from an ancient but surviving Chinese perspective, was that non-Chinese are barbarians in the fullest, most un-politically-correct meaning of the term. This historical episode is also an excellent illustration of how China is not, and has not been, monolithic: the Emperor, the

---

2   Those who seek a deeper dive into modern Chinese history would be hard pressed to find a better place to start than Jonathan Spence's *The Search for Modern China* (2012).

Son of Heaven (皇帝), was more sympathetic to Buddhism, a foreign religion than to his Confucian official.[3]

Today, China finds itself in a similar posture. Instead of Buddhism, the barbarian ideas at its gates include globalization, free market economics, and human rights. At every level of society and politics there is an unsettling struggle over what it means to be Chinese. The past century has witnessed convulsive change unprecedented in the nation's history. It is sobering to reflect that the reform era in China (approximately 1979 to the present) has been longer by over a decade than the period when the Communist Party ruled over an exclusively state-owned economy (1949 to approximately 1979). Communism, it should be emphasized, was itself a barbarian idea emanating mostly from the former Soviet Union which, until recent decades, maintained a sizable physical presence within China to match its political influence. The foreign origin of communism is precisely why so many Chinese leaders and scholars continue to emphasize the "Chinese characteristics" of its implementation in China (Xi, 2014), just as today its adoption of capitalism and free markets is also punctuated with the phase "with Chinese characteristics." In the early stages of the reform era, the transformative Chinese leader Deng Xiaoping declared that "to get rich is glorious," kick-starting an extraordinary period of economic growth that has made China into the world's second-largest economy with a GDP of over $13 trillion, trailing only the United States (albeit with a far larger population). China has embraced its own state-dominated form of free market economics, enjoying an impressive rate of annual economic growth over five decades—in some years exceeding 10 percent. As a result, hundreds of millions have been lifted out of poverty, although it bears emphasizing that hundreds of millions more remain below the World Bank's definition of the poverty line.

On 1 October 1949, Mao Zedong stood at the Gate of Heavenly Peace overlooking Tiananmen Square, the spot where for centuries emperors had addressed their subjects, and declared that "the Chinese people have stood

---

3   A note on language and script: in the rest of the book, we will use the Hànyǔ Pīnyīn (or just "pinyin") system to represent the pronunciation of Mandarin Chinese. We will also typically give Chinese characters—especially when a key term is first introduced. We will use traditional (more complex) characters even though simplified characters are the norm in the PRC. This is in part because of our emphasis on classic texts, but also because it is easier to infer simplified characters from traditional characters than vice-versa. For widely-known names of people and places, we will write them without tones, in the forms most commonly seen in the West (Xi Jinping, Shanghai, etc.).

up." The founding of the People's Republic of China marked the end of a century of humiliation when this proud and ancient nation was occupied by foreigners, first by Europeans in the 19th century and finally by Japan during the Second World War. A huge part of the explanation for why anti-foreign attitudes persist in modern China is how poorly China fared at the hands of foreign powers in the 19th and 20th centuries. After—and it bears repeating—*thousands* of years of sovereignty and apparent dominance of the world around it, China suffered embarrassing military, economic and legal defeats as well as social instability (which is anathema to Chinese notions of good government) at the hands of the foreigners during the 19th-century Opium Wars with the British as well as the Boxer Protocol, and the Sino-Japanese wars of the 1890s and 1930s–40s. The latter included the Japanese occupation of much of eastern and north-eastern China. This is in addition to internal rebellions whose origins included influences from outside China, such as the Taiping Rebellion (1850–1864), a pseudo-Christian religious movement that controlled much of southern China for nearly 14 years and resulted in the destruction of six hundred cities and the deaths of twenty million. In 1997, China reacquired Hong Kong from the United Kingdom, ending another humiliating chapter in its history. When the Olympic cauldron rose into the night sky above Beijing's National Stadium on 8 August 2008, China completed another momentous step in recapturing its former glory and emergence as a global power.

China has had its share of setbacks and challenges that threaten to undermine its progress. When things go wrong in China, a country where hundreds of millions of people still live on the edge of subsistence, they can go very wrong. In the late 1950s and early 1960s, Chairman Mao Zedong's Great Leap Forward promised that, by sheer will, China could speedily transform itself from a feudal rural economy to an industrialized nation. Farm workers were diverted to a series of mostly unsuccessful industrial work projects. The result was disastrous; an estimated 30 million people died of famine when agricultural production fell short of overly optimistic economic forecasts generated by the need to cater to Mao's political whim. Millions more suffered extreme degradation, humiliation, forced labor, and physical abuse during Mao's so-called Cultural Revolution of the 1960s.

After its economic opening to the West in the early 1980s, the Chinese government cleverly played overeager foreign investors against each other. "China is a big piece of cake," trade negotiator Wu Yi declared then, "and those who come first will get the biggest slice." American and European firms attempted to elbow each other aside to get into the Chinese market early and gain access to its manufacturing base and its billion-plus consumers. These companies met with varying levels of success. The tech sector well illustrates the full panoply of results achieved by foreign suitors. Some, like Apple, established manufacturing relationships (most notably through Foxconn) that helped to drive explosive global growth and make it the most valuable company and brand in the world. However, others like Google and Facebook remain mired in an endlessly frustrating processes of attempting to adapt their business models and values for the Chinese environment. Mark Zuckerberg's failure to successfully introduce Facebook into China was punctuated by his humiliating request for President Xi Jinping to offer a Chinese name for his soon-to-be-born first child. As the *New York Times* wryly observed, this was a "privilege reserved for older relatives, or sometimes a fortune teller." Mr. Xi quickly rejected the request (Mozur, Scott, & Isaac, 2017). Even Apple, it should be said, has had limited success in penetrating the Chinese smartphone market, with only a 5 percent share, with the domestic market leader Huawei controlling close to half.

One well-worn trope about the China Century needing revision concerns China's technological backwardness. Dating back decades to the reform efforts of Deng Xiaoping, when science and technological development formed key pillars of his "four modernizations," China has deliberately followed a program of technology transfer from the West. Sometimes this has been accomplished by trading access to the Chinese markets as a *quid pro quo* for sharing technological knowhow. In the case of the networking giant Cisco, this devil's bargain resulted in empowerment of what has become its most formidable global rival, Huawei. Often the technology "transfer" took the form of the outright theft of foreign trade secrets and other intellectual property. This kind of activity shows little signs of abating. In 2020, the chair of Harvard University's Chemistry and Chemical Biology Department along with two Chinese nationals were arrested and charged by the US Department of Justice with aiding the Chinese government by stealing intellectual property related to nanotechnology that was created in federally funded labs (Department of Justice: Office of Public Affairs, 2020).

China is no longer the technological neophyte it was at the beginning of the reform era. The technology transfer game is not simply one-sided anymore. China's Tencent has surpassed Facebook in market valuation. Part of the reason is that Tencent's WeChat is a more robust and user-friendly millennial communication tool than Facebook's Messenger (Aston, 2010, Ames & Rosemont, 1998). Many leading global companies are today investing in China to take advantage of a highly educated young workforce and burgeoning technological innovation hubs (Knight, 2018, Rogin, 2019). One sign that China's technological workers rival the very best of Silicon Valley is that Google, which left China's search business in 2010 over censorship concerns, is now reentering China. Why? Because China has nearly 800 million internet users? The real answer would probably surprise most Westerners. Google is returning to China because of its cutting-edge AI scientific knowledge and research (The Washington Post, 2018). At a recent annual conference of the Association for the Advancement of Artificial Intelligence, 23 percent of the presenters were Chinese—up from 10 percent in 2012. Thirty-four percent were from the United States, down from 41 percent. Fei-Fei Li, chief scientist of Google's Cloud, AI, and Machine Learning unit, proclaimed that "science has no borders . . . we want to work with the best AI talent, wherever that talent is." The borderless technology company envisioned by Fei-Fei Li has gotten a further boost in the wake of COVID-19 when technology companies like Facebook and Twitter announced that they would allow their employees to work remotely—in Twitter's case, permanently.

Yet another outdated trope about the China Century in need of revision is that China's economic ambitions are focused exclusively on low-wage manufacturing for export. Its ambitions are now global and its own investments are looking increasingly outward, most conspicuously through the "belt and road" initiative. In the United States, the Obama administration, aware of this emerging geopolitical threat, attempted to counteract China's soft power rise by proposing the Trans-Pacific Partnership (TPP), a 12-nation free trade pact with Australia, Brunei, Canada, Chile, Japan, Malaysia, Mexico, New Zealand, Peru, Singapore, and Vietnam. However, in a shortsighted move, the TPP was leveled by then-President Trump three days after he took office. With characteristic blunderbuss, Trump called the TPP a "rape of our country," but in truth he was making a major geopolitical miscalculation by reversing Obama's thoughtfully executed "pivot to Asia."

In all its complexity, with all its contradictions and challenges, the China Century presents the West with the potential for collaborative progress. For Westerners to fully seize the opportunity, however, they must learn to communicate more effectively with their Chinese counterparts, and to accomplish this they need to understand the deep layers of Chinese civilization, history, and thought that we describe and illustrate in this book.

1.4 The shadow of Tiananmen: economic reform and human rights

Through many Western eyes there has been a dark shadow over China's economic rise. The often-brutal authoritarian rule of the Communist Party has been responsible for some of the most pervasive and significant human rights violations the modern world has witnessed. Westerners of a certain age will never forget the searing images of China in June 1989: students occupying Tiananmen Square and erecting the Goddess of Democracy; these same students and sympathetic workers being slaughtered in the streets by People's Liberation Army soldiers; and a brave, solitary man defiantly standing in front of a stream of rolling tanks. For many Westerners, no matter how prosperous and powerful China has become, the dark legacy of Tiananmen will always define it. This impression is deepened by the fact that Chinese history books and websites are not permitted to discuss those events. Even today, for labor advocates the factory floors of China are an important battleground for global worker rights. Other human rights concerns include issues such as political repression, internet censorship, the use of facial recognition and artificial intelligence technology to keep track of and control citizens, and the territorial and cultural assaults on Tibetans and Uighurs. The Hong Kong turmoil of 2019 and 2020 was eerily reminiscent of Tiananmen Square, with hundreds of thousands taking to the streets in a quest for greater democracy and self-determination while the police and military mobilized ominously to quell the protests. The future of Hong Kong and the potential for violence and disorder to spill over into mainland China are as unpredictable as they are worrisome. Once more, calls for democracy and human rights seem headed for a showdown with an authoritarian regime bent on holding onto power at all costs.

Western business leaders find themselves reluctantly on the frontlines of these human rights struggles. There are today powerful global expectations coming from diverse directions that companies have significant responsibilities to address human rights violations. The ideas we discuss in this book about traditional Chinese culture present a paradox for human rights advocates. On the one hand, as we shall see, much of traditional Chinese culture and ethics is at odds with modern, Western conceptions of human rights. At the same time, in trying to implement global human rights standards, knowledge of traditional normative concepts and foundational values is indispensable for achieving progress on human rights.

When China first opened up its economy to the West, many observers—including one of the authors of this book—were hopeful that economic transformation would lead to the eventual emergence of democratic and human rights values (Santoro, 2000). Indeed, one of the key premises of China's admission into the World Trade Organization for many was that this transformation would at least incrementally occur. It is understandable that some might now have buyer's remorse about "normalizing" trade relations with China. The economic and socio-economic fallout for those working in manufacturing jobs has been more devastating than was expected, particularly in regions like the American Midwest. Conversely, the effect on social and political reform in China has been less pronounced than hoped for.

China has proven to be quite resistant to political change, even as its economy has transformed and its economic interactions with the rest of the world have increased. A number of factors have contributed to this persistence. First, it cannot be denied that the Communist Party has been nimble and effective in retaining power by coopting potential forces of change and continuing to exert control over the economy. To be sure, some areas of the economy, most notably social media, are proving to be not so easy for the Party to control (Jiang, 2016, pp. 139–144). However, for the most part, the Party rules over the economy with a heavy hand. Because the "free market" is not really free but rather subjected to strong government control, it should come as no surprise that these not-so-free markets have not led ineluctably toward democratization and dramatic human rights improvements. A second reason that economic transformation has had limited impact on political and social transformation is that Western companies have failed, for the most part, to stand up for values like the rule of law and economic rights that underpin both free markets and free societies (Santoro, 2009). As a result, the West missed the opportunity in the early stages of the reform era to help shape the business ethics environment in China, as well as its social and political development. At this point in time, Western or "barbarian" influence over China's future is highly limited. What narrow potential for influence remains can be, we will argue, significantly enhanced by understanding and applying normative concepts and foundational values of traditional Chinese culture. As we shall emphasize time and again in this book, the point of Westerners becoming familiar with this traditional culture is not to "go native," but rather to become more effective in achieving their own commercial, business ethics, and human rights objectives.

1.5 COVID-19: China and the West reset their relationship

The "Chinese Century" began as a tsunami of cheap manufactured exports overwhelming Western industry and displacing blue-collar workers. The steep social price of economic disruption in the industrial heartlands of the United States and Europe continue to unfold tragically in the form of persistent unemployment and an opioid crisis tearing apart families and communities. Westerners who focus solely on the "cheap labor" aspects of China's rise are, however, missing a momentous emerging story. In the third decade of the 21st century, China poses a more complex and deep-rooted challenge to the West. China has for some time been playing a "great game" deeply underappreciated by many in the West, quietly amassing broader economic prowess and "soft power" through its "belt and road" initiative consisting of carefully targeted and executed trade and infrastructure investments in over 126 countries and 29 international organizations spanning Asia, the Middle East, Latin America, Africa, and Europe. As a result, it has achieved geopolitical influence that arguably has surpassed that of the United States. Certainly, this is so in the United Nations simply by virtue of the growing number of countries falling increasingly under China's economic sway.

In 2020, the global COVID-19 pandemic revealed (to the surprise of some) the extent of China's influence over international institutions and how deeply interconnected China is to the rest of the world's economies. In April, then-President Trump halted funding to the World Health Organization (WHO). Two months later he announced that the United States would withdraw from the WHO altogether. He did so after being surprised by the fact that the United States sent ten times ($893 million) more money to the WHO than did China ($86 million) but that nevertheless the organization is "very, very China-centric." He should not have been surprised. Ethiopia, home of WHO Director-General Tedros Adhanom, offers an illustrative example of the influence China has purchased through its belt and road initiative.

Ethiopia owes half (estimated to be over $12 billion) of its external debt to China, including funding for a $475 million light railway system in the capital, Addis Ababa, and a $4 billion railway from the capital to Djibouti. While there has been no suggestion that Mr. Adhanom—a malaria researcher with a Ph.D. in community health from the University of Nottingham—has profited from these investments, it would be naïve to think that China's support did not impact his election to Director-General in 2017. It would also be naïve, however, to think that China is not exerting ongoing influence within the WHO as it does throughout the UN, greased by its "soft power" investments throughout the world. In a hard-fought election among member states with political jockeying behind the scenes, Mr. Adhanom won by garnering 133 out of 185 votes, becoming the first non-medical doctor and the first African to ascend to the post. Whether China effectively bought a COVID-19 hall pass from the WHO is something we will likely never know. The fact that Mr. Adhanom—after meeting with Chinese leaders in January 2020—praised China's containment efforts, declared shortly thereafter that it was unnecessary to restrict international trade and travel, and was late to label COVID-19 a global pandemic, might as easily be attributed to mistaken judgment as undue influence.

Another "revelation" of the COVID-19 pandemic was the extent to which global supply chains were dependent on Chinese manufacturing. When the initial xenophobia over the origins of the virus in the city of Wuhan temporarily subsided, many in the West fully understood for the first time how the supply chain for everything from iPhones and televisions to Tylenol and hospital ventilators are dependent on Chinese exports. The resultant conversation about the quality, reliability, and safety of this supply chain raised many troubling questions. Owing to the health concerns that sparked the conversation, Western dependence on China's manufacture of "active pharmaceutical ingredients" (APIs) in the drug supply was particularly singled out by political leaders. Two California members of the US Congress went so far as to call reliance on China for API and the "rare earth minerals" that go into high-tech commercial and military products a "national security" issue (Eshoo & Schiff, 2019).

While it is an understandable instinct to correct strategic overreliance on a China-dominant supply chain in key sectors, the sudden desire to sever supply relationships built up over decades has met with considerable resistance from multinational corporations. PhRMA, a trade organization representing some of the largest pharmaceutical companies and the US Chamber of Commerce, among others, have lobbied intensively against government efforts to reduce reliance on China. They argue that over the course of decades China's export economy has become inextricably bound to the rest of the world and that it would be unwise and inefficient to attempt to unravel longstanding supply arrangements. In the wake of the COVID-19 pandemic, however, there is likely to be increasing scrutiny from regulators about assuring the integrity of the supply chain on a host of issues ranging from safety and quality to human rights. In August 2020, then-President Trump went so far as to issue an executive order instructing the federal government to buy and give preference to drugs and supplies made in the United States. The calls to bring at least some manufacturing in key strategic sectors back to Europe or the United States are likely to continue in the Biden administration. The post-COVID-19 pressure to reduce over-reliance on China in supply chains will precipitate a host of conversations about difficult subjects that have been on the backburner for many global companies. It is unclear how these conversations will unfold in the United States and Europe now that Donald Trump is no longer in power. One fact will, however, remain true in the Biden era. Significant progress on safety, quality, and human rights will require more effective communication and relationship-building, which can be enhanced by—and we believe depends on—mastery of the essentials of traditional Chinese culture we present in this book.

1.6 The durability of traditional Chinese culture in contemporary China: or, why foreign business executives should take page from Xi Jinping's playbook

References to traditional Chinese culture are ubiquitous even in what are seemingly the most modern of contemporary economic and political interactions. In May 2020, for example, as COVID-19-related anti-China sentiment was reaching a fever pitch in the United States, diplomat Xie Feng penned a plaintive op-ed in the *Wall Street Journal* expressing China's frustrations over foreign attempts to take advantage of the pandemic by demanding reparations (Xie, 2020). Xie Feng attempted to bolster his argument by quoting a Chinese proverb which itself is a thinly veiled reference to Confucius: "a gentleman pursues wealth in a righteous way" (Confucius, 1998, pp. 89–90, 113). Confucius famously criticized displays of wealth, and is reported to

have said that "gentlemen" or civilized, sophisticated, and ethically cultivated people, understand rightness while small or "petty" people understand profit (Confucius, 1998, p. 92). Other, more disparaging remarks about
wealth, its excessive accumulation and display are scattered throughout the
Confucian *Analects* (Confucius, 1998, pp. 91, 145). These remarks indicate
that material riches, in and of themselves, are not what the civilized, cultivated person values in life.

Remarkably, in a piece placed in perhaps the most traditional Western business news outlet designed to advance diplomatic relations and influence global
opinion, Xie Feng explains his country's worldview through a 2,000-year-old
proverb uttered by the most distinctively Chinese cultural icon. What was he
trying to say about China's worldview that required reference to an ancient
proverb? Try as he might to be diplomatic, Xie Feng was giving a subtle dig
to the effect that Chinese ethical ideals are high-minded and cultivated, in
contrast with the behavior of some Western nations claiming that China is to
blame for the origin of the virus and its spread. To simplify, the implication
is that cultivated (Chinese) people are civilized, unlike Western "barbarians"
who try to shift responsibility from themselves by pointing fingers at others,
like children do on a playground. A second implication is that Chinese ethics
and ideals are older, and therefore more venerable. Again, simplifying somewhat, the message is: "by the way, we knew how to behave properly a long
time ago." Moreover, a smattering of remarks in the article imply Chinese
intellectual and cultural superiority, for example: "China took a 'closed-book
exam,' with uplifting results that have informed other countries' decision-
making in the 'open-book tests' that followed" (Xie, 2020). This is also,
almost certainly, an implicit request for respect from Western nations.

Xie Feng makes several other rhetorical moves that merit attention, if
we are to understand Chinese perspectives on China-West tensions underscored by COVID-19. In the same paragraph as the thinly veiled reference to
Confucius, the author mentions the "Boxer Indemnity." This is a reference
to the Protocol, signed at the end of the Boxer Rebellion, 1899–1901. It was
signed by the Chinese government on one side, and by Russia, six European
nations, and the United States on the other. According to the Protocol, the
Chinese government agreed to pay roughly 18,000 metric tons of silver to
the Western powers and punish its own citizens for crimes against Western
powers occurring on Chinese soil, which one would normally assume to be
outside the jurisdiction of Western laws (Spence, 2012).

Mention of the Boxer Indemnity serves more broadly as a reminder of the Century of Humiliation (1840s–1940s), during which China suffered repeated economic, military, and political defeats at foreign hands. No doubt, the author sees China as unjustly accused by Westerners of inventing or scattering the virus, and instinctively wants to "save face" by pointing out China's relative success at stemming the spread of the virus. Finally, the author repeatedly suggests that a more cooperative approach is more likely to save lives—that is, an "us-versus-COVID-19" outlook rather than the prevailing West-versus-China outlook. A spirit of cooperation (even if largely formal or even feigned at first) and an avoidance of us-versus-them rhetoric, even in the face of competition (especially in business), are foundational values of traditional Chinese culture that we will emphasize throughout this book.

As our deconstruction of Xie Feng's op-ed illustrates, traditional Chinese culture is quite often just below the surface of contemporary interactions with the West, resonating in subtle ways and sometimes requiring careful attention to effectively understand and communicate. Of course, anyone who has traveled to China might rightly and quite obviously observe that not everyone thinks in the same way. We are certainly appreciative of such well-founded skepticism about our project. The idea of 1.4 billion people thinking the same way about ethics would seem a dubious starting proposition. Would anyone claim all Americans or Russians think alike? Indeed, quite a number of Chinese citizens whom we approached that are Western-educated or have had extensive exposure to foreigners understandably resented any notions that they can be pigeon-holed or caricatured in a simplistic manner, particularly one that would reduce them to embodying millennia-old tomes they might have read as youths in school. We certainly do not wish to do anything of the sort in this book. Rather, our argument is that the classics are still highly relevant to modern Chinese mores and sensibilities, not that they dominate or dictate the outlook of every Chinese citizen on every issue.

We are also appreciative of the fact that, as in other societies, there are many layers and substrata of cultures that in contemporary settings, and over the course of history, have interacted with and helped to shape the social and cultural legacy of the classics. Indeed, the precise nature of values associated with traditional Chinese culture has been a matter of considerable debate and controversy for millennia. Through the centuries, for example, Confucius and the teachings attributed to him have been adopted, interpreted, and reinvented in an almost endless cycle of reform and return to tradition to suit the needs of the day (Nylan & Wilson, 2010). Moreover, there have been many foreign influences on "traditional" culture, as for example during the Jurchen Jin, Mongolian Yuan, and Manchu Qing dynasties. Moreover, we are also mindful that the classics of Chinese literature and philosophy can hardly be expected to provide a full picture of who a modern Chinese person is or how they might behave. What follows is no substitute for immersing yourself in pop culture, art, or contemporary political discourse. It should be read as but one part—but we will argue an indispensable and oft-overlooked one—of a complex picture needed to understand and operate effectively in contemporary China. The fundamental premise of this book is that the classics still matter in contemporary Chinese business. For example, Confucius and Sun Tzu (more accurately written "Sunzi") continue to resonate in contemporary Chinese business and ethics in ways that Homer and Virgil do not in the West (Ames and Rosemont 1998, Sunzi, 2011). Even if not literally read by everyone, the values are taught at home and in school. Globalization, free market economics, and human rights are new ideas being introduced into China whose impact on its cultural traditions will, in the fullness of time, unfold. Whatever the ultimate influence of these foreign ideas will be, the normative concepts and fundamental values transmitted in the classics will continue to exert significant influence.

In the interest of sticking to our pledge not to caricature Chinese mindsets, we hasten to add that the degree to which traditional values are going to characterize and affect the behavior of any particular Chinese counterpart is going to be on a spectrum. If you are sitting across the table from a Beida (Peking University) graduate with an MBA from Harvard and five years of work experience at Morgan Stanley, they are more likely to have taken the same negotiations course you took in school and there is very likely to be less cultural residue from having read the classics as a youth in school (very likely, but not absolutely so). On the other hand, if you are across the table from a government official or factory manager with little exposure to Western education, these kinds of mental frameworks could be more significant. The point of studying the Chinese classics is not to create a new kind of blunder where a Westerner sees a traditional mindset in every encounter. This would be as dysfunctional as ignoring the residues of traditional culture when they do appear in contemporary business. The point of this book is to raise fluency in thinking through that culture, recognize how it might color a particular encounter or business proposition, and learn to be agile in how you respond. (As we have noted, the importance of "agility" in navigating Chinese culture is a foundational theme we develop in this book.)

Contemporary Chinese political leaders are keenly aware of the power of appeal to traditional values. This was not always the case in the Communist Party. During the Cultural Revolution in the 1960s and 70s, Mao Zedong systematically and brutally attempted to purge the country of its millennia-old traditional culture. Even in the early years of reform, the Party stressed modernization and change over continuity, with sanguinity over the cultural consequences. "There are those who say we should not open our windows, because open windows let in flies and other insects," Deng Xiaoping remarked in October 1985. "They want the windows to stay closed, so we all expire from lack of air. But we say, 'Open the windows, breathe the fresh air and at the same time fight the flies and insects'" (Church, 1986). Today, however, the country's leaders have moved decisively to embrace, reinterpret, and sometimes twist the tenets of traditional culture to advance their agendas.

President Xi Jinping has called traditional culture the "foundation" and "wellspring" of the Party's values (Xi, 2014). In 2015, Xi went so far as to publish his own version of Mao's *Little Red Book* that was entitled *"Classical Aphorisms by Xi Jinping,"* which quotes from Confucius, Mencius, and Laozi, among others, and dubiously attempts to portray the authoritarian Xi as a paragon of traditional Chinese values (ChinaDaily, 2015). Xi's "discovery" of the classics is a powerful tell-tale of their persistent importance. Westerners would be well advised to take a cue from him if they want to be effective when doing business in China. Put simply, if China's paramount leader Xi Jinping thinks it is important to invoke traditional ethical values to persuade the Chinese people about his ideas, then Westerners should appreciate their value in winning friends and influencing people. In the next chapter, we offer a roadmap for doing so.

References

Adler, J. (2002). *Chinese religious traditions*. London: Laurence King Publishing.

Ames, R., & Rosemont, H. (1998). *The analects of Confucius*. New York: Random House.

Aston, A. (2010, December 7). 7 technologies where china has the US beat. *GreenBiz*. Retrieved December 15, 2019, from www.greenbiz.com/blog/2010/12/07/7-technologies-where-china-has-us-beat

Benn, J. A. (2015). *Tea in China: A religious and cultural history.* Honolulu: University of Hawai'i Press.

ChinaDaily. (2015, March 2). Chinese president Xi Jinping's quotes in a book. *ChinaDaily.com.cn.* Retrieved from www.chinadaily.com.cn/culture/2015-03/02/content_19695291.htm

Church, G. G. (1986, January 6). China: Old wound Deng Xiaoping. *Time.*

Confucius, K. (1998). *The analects of Confucius: A philosophical translation* (R. T. Ames & H. Rosemont, Trans.). New York: Random House.

Department of Justice: Office of Public Affairs. (2020, January 28). *Harvard University professor and two Chinese nationals charged in three separate china related cases.* Retrieved from www.justice.gov/opa/pr/harvard-university-professor-and-two-chinese-nationals-charged-three-separate-china-related

Donaldson, T. (1996). Values in tension: Business away from home. *Harard Business Review.* Retrieved June 19, 2020, from https://hbr.org/1996/09/values-in-tension-ethics-away-from-home

Eshoo, A. G., & Schiff, A. B. (2019, September 10). China's grip on pharmaceutical drugs is a national security issue. *Washington Post.* Retrieved from www.washingtonpost.com/opinions/we-rely-on-china-for-pharmaceutical-drugs-thats-a-security-threat/2019/09/10/5f35e1ce-d3ec-11e9-9343-40db57cf6abd_story.html

Hofstede, G. (1994). The business of international business is culture. *International Business Review,* 1–14.

Hu, X., Xiaohua Chen, S., Zhang, L., Yu, F., Peng, K., & Liu, L. (2018, November 6). Do Chinese traditional and modern cultures affect young adults moral priorities? *Frontiers in Psychology,* 9.

Jiang, M. (2016, January). Chinese internet business and human rights. *Business and Human Rights Journal,* 1(1), 139–144.

Kamm, J. (2020, April 11). Author Interview.

Knight, W. (2018, December 19). China vs. the US: Who wins and who loses. *MIT Technology Review.* Retrieved December 15, 2019, from www.technologyreview.com/s/612603/china-vs-the-us-who-wins-and-who-loses/

Mozur, P., Scott, M., & Isaac, M. (2017, September). Facebook faces a new world as officials rein in a wild web. *The New York Times.*

Nylan, M., & Wilson, T. (2010). *Lives of Confucius: Civilizations greatest sage through the ages.* New York: Crown Publishing Group.

Roetz, H. (2009). *What it means to take Chinese ethics seriously* (J. T. Kam-Por Yu, Ed.). Albany: SUNY Press.

Rogin, J. (2019, March 7). China is racing ahead of the United States on blockchain. *The Washington Post*. Retrieved December 15, 2019, from www. washingtonpost.com/opinions/global-opinions/china-is-racing-ahead-of-the-united-states-on-blockchain/2019/03/07/c1e7776a-4116-11e9-9361-301ffb5bd5e6_story.html

Santoro, M. A. (2000). *Profits and principle: Global capitalism and human rights in China*. Ithaca, NY: Cornell University Press.

Santoro, M. A. (2009). *China 2020: How Western business can—and should—influence social and political change in the coming decade*. Ithaca, NY: Cornell University Press.

Sigley, G. (2015). Tea and China's rise: Tea, nationalism, and culture in the 21st century. *International Communication of Chinese Culture, 2*, 319–341.

Spence, J. D. (2012). *The search for modern China* (3rd ed.). New York: Norton.

Stone, B. (2020, April 19). Author Interview.

Sunzi. (2011). *The art of war* (P. J. Ivanhoe, Trans.). Indianapolis: Hackett.

The Washington Post. (2018, July 20). China overtakes US in quantity of AI research. Retrieved December 15, 2019, from www.scmp.com/lifestyle/article/2029101/china-has-now-eclipsed-us-quantity-ai-research

Wu-Chi, L. (1990). *An introduction to Chinese literature*. Westport, CT: Praeger.

Xi, J. (2014). *The governance of China* (Vol. 1–2). Beijing: Foreign Languages Press.

Xie, F. (2020, May 12). China wants to help the world fight coronavirus. *The Wall Street Journal*. Retrieved from www.wsj.com/articles/china-wants-to-help-the-world-fight-coronavirus-11589322607

2

AN ETHICAL TRIAD FOR UNDERSTANDING TRADITIONAL CHINESE CULTURE

Context-First, Interconnectedness, and Awareness—and how they can be used to protect intellectual property

In this chapter we present a framework for helping Western minds access and engage with traditional Chinese ways of thinking and acting about ethics and business. Our primer comprises three interrelated foundational principles—Context-First, Interconnectedness, and Awareness—that we call the Ethical Triad for Understanding Traditional Chinese Culture (see Figure 2.1). After setting forth our framework, we apply it to one of the most vexing ethical issues foreign businesses face in China—the protection of intellectual property (IP). Even though, as we shall see, there is a significant cultural divide in the way China and the West view the law of intellectual property, our Ethical Triad enables effective communication and relationship-building tools for protecting patents, copyrights, trademarks, and other forms of IP.

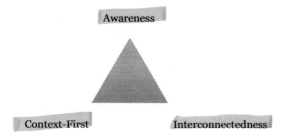

Figure 2.1 An Ethical Triad for understanding traditional Chinese culture

2.1 Context-First vs. Rules-First: fundamental differences in Chinese vs. Western ethical thinking

A critical first step toward "getting inside" Chinese thinking and perspectives on ethics and business is to understand a distinction in how different global thought traditions approach ethics from the very outset. There is a fundamentally different approach in China (and much of East Asia) as to what ethics is and how it works than there is in the West. Context—the real-world situation one occupies—plays a larger role in Chinese ethical decision-making than in the West.

In much of the West, especially in Western Europe and the United States, ethics is typically presented and perceived as being about universal rules that everyone must follow (Rosemont, 1988, Nisbett, 2003, Shun & Wong, 2004). Such rules are "disinterested" in the sense that they apply to every person in the same way and without personal favoritism (Frankena, 1988). For example, although on very different grounds, both Kantian and Utilitarian frameworks hold that all persons are due the same ethical consideration. Thus, the Western starting point of ethics is: "there are rules of behavior, which apply to everyone, such that we all need to learn and follow them."[4]

---

4   Throughout the book, references are made to "rules," "principles," and "values," where each term can have subtly different connotations. Rules are more cut-and-dry directives that allow very little interpretation, whereas principles are broader and allow for some interpretation as one applies them in specific situations. Values are the broadest, allowing for significant interpretation when applied. From that perspective, it would be more accurate to describe Western approaches to ethics as "principle-first" rather than "rule-first," but we have settled on the latter in part because, as we will argue later, whether or not "principle-first" or "rule-first" is more accurate, the starting-points of Western ethics are generally *presented* as more like rules, especially to children, students, and even employees.

To be sure, context is relevant as well—one must be able to apply rules of behavior to specific situations in which one finds oneself—but rules come first. Chinese ethics, by contrast, tend to be deeply skeptical of universal or absolute rules that apply to everyone. Instead, Chinese moral reasoning emphasizes particular values such as the closeness of personal relationships, respecting hierarchies, and benevolence toward those with whom one has close relations, as well as the networks of relationships within which those values are applied (Pitta, Fung, & Isberg, 1999).[5] In other words, disinterestedness, a bedrock principle of Western ethics, is the very opposite of the bedrock principles of personal connections and networks that underlay traditional Chinese ethics. Disinterestedness implies a lack of person-specific orientation that is central to Chinese ethics.

It is typical in much of the West for children to be taught ethics roughly as follows. Basic rules such as "don't lie" and "don't steal" are presented as universal maxims applying to everyone. Anyone who has been around Western children for any period of time will have seen situations where a child sees an adult breaking some such rule—perhaps uttering a white lie to smooth over a social situation and avoid causing someone else embarrassment. Depending on parenting style, the child may call out the adult by saying "but you lied," apparently thinking that the adult has broken their own rule. Our point is not whether the adult did (or did not) lie, but rather how ethics were evidently presented to, and understood by, the child. Ethics is typically presented and understood in terms of learning rules, and then learning when it may be permissible to break or creatively interpret those rules depending on specific situations and contexts.

In typical business ethics textbooks, this Rules-First approach continues. Students are again taught that the foundations of ethics comprise rules that apply to everyone. Examples include the Utilitarian "act so as to maximize happiness and minimize suffering," or the Kantian "act in such a way that you could rationally will anyone to act in that way." One then turns to

---

5   Sociologists and other behavioral scientists discuss "higher- versus lower-context" cultures and languages, where context plays a relatively greater or lesser role in interpreting everyday speech and behavior. Not just texts, but Chinese culture and languages, such as Mandarin, are themselves viewed by anthropologists, sociologists, and linguists as "high context." To say a language or culture is "high context" means that to correctly interpret a speaker, especially in everyday talking and writing, one must typically understand the context of speech as well as cultural connotations of words, including their historical associations (Hall, 1959, 1977, He, 2016).

specific situations (in business ethics often in the form of cases) to learn how to apply these universal maxims in context.

To be clear, we are not making an all-or-nothing claim about rules versus context in Western approaches to ethics. We claim neither that all classes and texts work this way, nor that all parents raise children in a certain way, nor that all Western ethical frameworks fit this pattern. We also do not claim that Western ethics is only about universal maxims and never about context. Rather, the basic point we are trying to make is that the general Western mindset regarding ethics is rules first, context second. Aristotelian Virtue Ethics may be a partial exception insofar as it emphasizes habits of character over specific rules or maxims. Indeed, many of the most successful business ethics training programs within Western companies are those that instill fundamental corporate values such as integrity or honesty—rather than rules—and then train employees in how to apply those values in varying concrete situations in which they may find themselves (Sekerka, 2009, pp. 77–95, 2018). These value-based or, as they are sometimes called, "principle-based" approaches have been shown to be more successful at cultivating ethical behavior and reducing ethical failures than stricter "rule-based" compliance training to "do this and don't do that" (Paine, 1994). That said, however, attempting to instill a consistent pattern of behavior in accordance with a virtue like integrity or honesty is still in some sense an instance of attempting to achieve adherence to a universal rule.

applied values rather than a list of do's & don'ts

The Ten Commandments of the Hebrew Bible (or "Old Testament") constitute a quintessential example of Rules-First ethics. Each commandment is a rule of behavior one must follow in order to avoid punishment. The Ten Commandments are presented, and often taught, as absolute. An example of how the Rules-First mode of ethical reasoning works in business is JP Morgan Chase Co.'s Code of Conduct. For many years it has featured a flowchart where, for an employee to determine whether some act is ethically permissible, they must ask if it passes certain tests that are transparently based on the maxims of standard (Western) ethical frameworks. Questions have recently included: "am I sure it would not cause loss or harm to our clients, customers, markets, shareholders or company," "would it be okay if everyone did it," and "am I sure I would not be uncomfortable or embarrassed if I read about it on the front page of the newspaper" (JP Morgan Chase & Co., 2015, p. 4). Respectively, these represent Utilitarian, Kantian, or "deontological" and virtue-theoretic frameworks, which are typically presented as core frameworks for ethics in business-ethics texts. Again, the starting point is learning to follow rules of behavior. Secondary evidence of the Rules-First mindset is that, in business contexts specifically, ethics and compliance are, more often than not, grouped together both in common parlance and in organizational structure.

Again, our claim is not that Western ethics ignores context, nor is our claim that there are no rules at all in Chinese ethics. However, there are sharp distinctions between the two approaches. To illustrate the differences in approach, consider a classic dilemma used in teaching ethics. You are in Nazi-controlled Germany and your Jewish friends are hiding in the basement. The Gestapo arrive and demand to know whether you are harboring any Jews. You are caught between two competing rules. On the one hand, one must not lie. However, if you tell the truth to the Gestapo, then you betray your friends and become complicit in their torture and probable deaths. Though perhaps Kant himself may not have agreed, standard Kantian thinking is that in this particular context, the rule not to lie is outweighed by the rule not to betray your friends to a regime that intends to murder them. This is an apt illustration that although context is relevant in Western ethical thinking, the rules are the starting place, and from there one learns how to interpret them in specific situations and contexts.

This notion of universal rules that apply equally to everyone, by contrast, does not make sense within Chinese culture contexts. To illustrate this, and what we mean by Context-First, we consider how Chinese ethics would work through the Friends-Gestapo dilemma. The starting-point would be the relationships that you, the decision-maker, have with the relevant groups. On the one hand are your friends with whom you have an established personal relationship that is so close and strong that you have hidden them in your basement. On the other hand, there are the authorities, with whom you have no personal relationship, who are doing their jobs serving a presumably temporary and certainly evil regime. In situations like these, and in general, personal relationships trump impersonal ones. From a Chinese perspective, the only relevant consideration regarding the authorities is to not get caught, which would endanger your friends' lives and expose your family to serious risk. Crucially, there is no real tension between established ethical rules or principles. A Chinese perspective on this case looks first at the specifics of this particular context, in this case at the specific relationships you have with the relevant parties—friends versus authorities. This is not to say that no principles or general rules are operative at all. There is one such implicit in the case—that personal relationships trump impersonal ones (a theme we will return to throughout this book). The point for our framework is that whereas the Western approach to the case started with general rules and then looked at context, the Chinese approach to the case started with the particulars of the context, and then moved to a general principle.

A Chinese analog of the Friend-Gestapo dilemma can be found in the Confucian *Analects* where a Duke converses with Confucius, here named "Kongzi," which is his family name "*Kǒng*" plus the honorific "*zi*," meaning "master":

> 13.18 The Duke of She said to Kongzi, "Among my people there is one we call 'Upright Gong.' When his father stole a sheep, he reported him to the authorities."
>
> Kongzi replied, "Among my people, those who we consider 'upright' are different from this: fathers cover up for their sons, and sons cover up for their fathers. 'Uprightness' is found in this." (Ivanhoe and Van Norden, 2005) .

As should now be apparent, what was true of Confucius' "my people" came to be true of Chinese people at large. Though the ultimate answer in this circumstance—do not tell the cops—is the same, the Context-First approach gets there by different ethical reasoning than the Rules-First approach. Here, and as became common in Chinese thinking about ethics, an overly rigid sense of uprightness—of moral rule-following such as the Duke describes—is actually thought to be harmful (Ivanhoe & Van Norden, 2005).

Another illustration of the importance of context, as it is built into Chinese ethics, can be found in a famous and oft-cited passage from the *Analects* where Confucius is seen giving very different answers to two students who ask the same question. This is an example of Context-First, because it illustrates how each student needs a different answer because of their personalities and their relationship to their teacher (Confucius). The "right" answer appears to vary, and is not determined just by the question, but also by who is asking the question. Indeed, to Chinese perspectives, it is immature and even naïve to suppose that the same question always receives the same answer. Here, "the Master" refers to Confucius, as it is known in Confucian circles that there is only one, while Zilu, Ran Qiu, and Zihua are three of his students.

11.22 Zilu asked, "Upon learning of something that needs to be done, should one immediately take care of it?"

The Master replied, "As long as one's father and elder brothers are still alive, how could one possibly take care of it immediately?"

[On a later occasion] Ran Qiu asked, "Upon learning of something that needs to be done, should one immediately take care of it?"

The Master replied, "Upon learning of it, you should immediately take care of it."

Zihua inquired, "When Zilu asked you whether or not one should immediately take care of something upon learning of it, you told him one should not, as long as one's father and elder brothers are still alive. When Ran Qiu asked the same question, however, you told him that one should immediately take care of it. I am confused, and humbly ask to have this explained to me."

The Master said, "Ran Qiu is overly cautious, and so I wished to urge him on. Zilu, on the other hand, is too impetuous, and so I sought to hold him back."

(Ivanhoe & Van Norden, 2005, pp. 31–32)

Here, Confucius' knowledge of the differing temperaments of the two students allows him to perceive that achieving good pedagogical outcomes requires giving different answers to the same question. That knowledge is important for helping the students progress in their own character development. Applying this to business, whom one is talking to can make a difference not only as to how one says things, but also as to what one says and what one is trying to achieve. A Westerner might object: good teachers sensitive to the varying needs of students in the East, West, and elsewhere will sometimes give students different answers to the same question. Again, we make no all-or-nothing claim that context is irrelevant to Western mindsets, only that it comes after the rules, and our point here is that this extends outside of teaching to business and ethics more broadly.

At this point, someone coming from a Western perspective might worry that the Context-First approach to ethics risks eviscerating ethics of its normative "bite." If it's all context, the thought goes, then there may be no real rhyme or reason in ethics. Who's to say what's ethically right, wrong, or appropriate in any given situation if context plays such a central role while rules take a back seat? The underlying—and very natural—worry is that, without rules, we descend into some form of relativism where there is no real ethical right or wrong. Our response to this skepticism is two-fold. First, we reiterate that "Context-First" does not mean "it's only context and nothing else." Rather, it means that the first step toward understanding ethics and ethical behavior is to understand how to read contexts, for instance as Confucius did in the previous example, by knowing the differing temperaments of his two students. Second, while the notion of an absolute rule that applies to everyone does not make sense in Chinese culture contexts, there are nonetheless guidelines—normative concepts and general values—that one learns to apply in varying ways depending on context, such as propriety, benevolence, and respect for hierarchies, all of which we will discuss in Chapter 5. As we shall see, these values and principles have real normative bite, it's just that their application depends first on context.

2.2 Interconnectedness: hurried executives vs. enduring partnerships

The second foundation of our Ethical Triad is "Interconnectedness." According to Chinese perspectives on ethics, to say that something is "just manners," "just superstition," or "just a local social or cultural norm" but not "real ethics" makes no sense. Those distinctions, often so carefully drawn in the West, do not apply in Chinese culture contexts. We call this "Interconnectedness." It means that the divisions between what counts as philosophy, religion, superstition, culture, and tradition are much fuzzier in China, and in much of East Asia, than they are in the West. A classic example is when visitors to China (or for that matter students in a Chinese culture or philosophy class) ask whether Confucius was a philosophical figure or a religious figure. Frustratingly to many Westerners, the answer is "yes." This is not because Confucius was somehow both Socrates and Jesus rolled into one, though it is sometimes said that Confucius' influence is comparable to that of Socrates and Jesus combined. Rather, to really understand the cryptic "yes" answer to an apparently "either-or" question, one must understand that religion and philosophy, as Western minds understand them, are not typically distinguishable in Chinese contexts. One must resist the expectation that Western concepts, or in this case Western distinctions, should always map perfectly onto non-Western cultures. For another example, Zen (禪, in Chinese, Chán) Buddhism is simultaneously religious and philosophical.

Instead of trying to export concepts, distinctions, and categories to cultural contexts in which they do not function well—effectively trying to fit a conceptual square peg into a round hole—we advocate taking up a new concept, Interconnectedness, and becoming familiar with applying it in Chinese culture contexts, specifically in business. An application of Interconnectedness may be familiar to those who have lived and/or done business in China: what is personal and what is business is not as clearly separated as is typical in the West. The Western catch-phrase "it's not personal, it's business" makes no sense in China. Consider the story told by Stefan Verstappen about "The Hurried Executive," an inexperienced American executive sent to China and given three days to negotiate a new contract with a supplier:

> The welcoming committee of bubbly smiling middle managers greeted him at the airport. He told them that he was on a tight schedule and that he would like to arrange an appointment the next day with company Executives. "Yes, Yes," the managers said as he was whisked to his hotel. At this point in the story . . . more experienced "China hands" . . . know . . . the executive had already made three mistakes. The next day the executive was picked up at the hotel by the welcoming committee and whisked off to tour the company's manufacturing facilities. Throughout the day, the executive kept asking when he could meet with the senior manager to start negotiations. They assured him that the meeting would occur shortly and meantime there were other places to visit. Exhausted, the executive returned to his room still without having started negotiations or even meeting the senior managers.
>
> On the third and final day of his stay, the executive was now in a panic. He only had a few hours left to negotiate a contract before his return flight. After desperate pleading with his welcoming committee, they finally assured him the senior manager would see him before he left. The welcoming committee picked up the executive to drive him to the airport and on the way, they also picked up a senior manager! With only minutes left to negotiate, the executive signed a contract that was highly unfavorable to his company.
>
> . . . The first mistake was to start discussing business right away; the second, believing that only one person in a Chinese company is in charge of making decisions; and the third, expecting quick results.
>
> (Verstappen, 2015)

Of the three mistakes, the first is most relevant to Interconnectedness. In an environment where business is personal, in part because there is no Western-style rule of law to effectively regulate business interactions, the Western executive needed to cultivate personal relationships with the Chinese partners before any meaningful business relationship could be built. (It is also worth noting that three days was quite an unrealistic timeframe for building such relationships.)

Further in the spirit of Interconnectedness, the story of The Hurried Executive is also an illustration of certain famous ideas from *The Art of War*. Typically, in situations like that of the story just recounted, Chinese managers and executives view themselves as out to negotiate the best terms for their firm, not to help the Western business executive promote the interests of their firm. While the Western perspective might be that of looking for partners, the more typical Chinese perspective will be that of ensuring as much competitive advantage as possible for one's own company. The Chinese middle managers in the story did just that by putting the Western executive in a panic to the point where he became willing to sign a contract unfavorable to his own company. In terms of *The Art of War*, the Chinese managers maneuvered the Western executive into "encircled terrain" where the Westerner was effectively trapped, such that there was only one way out if the executive was to have a contract signed before his flight left (Sunzi, 2011, pp. 73–74). The Western executive did not understand this mindset of Chinese business negotiation and, moreover, unbeknownst to him, he also failed to take *The Art of War*'s advice to make plans to avoid being put into such a position (i.e., to avoid being pushed onto "encircled terrain"). The Westerner not only failed to understand his opponent, he failed to understand that he had an opponent. In general, once in China, one only becomes partners (in a Western sense) once one has built personal relationships that in turn serve as a foundation for building business relations.

2.3 Ethical Awareness

The third foundational pillar of our framework for understanding Chinese ethical thought and practice is what we call "Ethical Awareness."[6] Ethical Awareness builds upon Context-First and Interconnectedness. Having

---

6   In calling it "Awareness" we are partly inspired by P. J. Ivanhoe (2013, pp. 72-84).

Awareness means having a sufficiently cultivated ethical "sixth-sense," that one can: recognize an ethical situation as being ethical; identify the ethically relevant factors of the situation; know which ethical values to apply given those factors; and then see how to put those principles into practice given the actual situation. Influential religio-philosophical traditions within Chinese culture, including ones that disagree on a great many things such as Confucianism and Daoism (also spelled "Taoism"), nevertheless agree on this point: one of the central components of ethical wisdom and ability is the cultivation of a kind of intuitive sense whereby one can read context and its intricacies so as to identify how to behave in ethically appropriate ways. This ability is Ethical Awareness.

By and large, Western approaches to ethics, especially as they are typically applied to business, do not place as high a value on cultivating an ethically trained intuitive or "sixth sense" as part of becoming an ethically cultivated person who can make more ethical decisions. In Chinese, and many East Asian culture contexts, exemplars of this intuitive sense are, in effect, "connoisseurs of ethics" in a way similar to music masters or chefs "just know" from learning and experience what sounds or flavors will go together.[7] An exception can be found in some forms of Virtue Ethics, for instance Aristotelianism, where the virtuous person has "practical wisdom" that allows them to "read" situations in such a way that they can distinguish virtuous from non-virtuous decisions. Indeed, the connection is not accidental: Confucius and his followers are often classified as virtue theorists, placing them in the same neighborhood of ethical theory as Aristotle (Van Norden, 2007, Angle & Slote, 2013).[8] Though different traditions have different ways of talking about it, and different background commitments, in this specific aspect of Awareness—the idea that ethically cultivated persons develop a trained intuitive sense of ethical situations—there is some commonality between Western and Chinese ethical frameworks.

Such a sense or intuition does not, however, play a key role in the other important Western frameworks typically employed in business ethics, such

---

7   This is simultaneously another instance of Interconnectedness: in this case, of ethics and aesthetics.

8   In contrast, Roger Ames and Henry Rosemont argue that Confucian ethics are not properly understood as a virtue ethics, but they do so on grounds consistent with our larger argument—that ultimately, Western virtue ethics like Aristotelianism promote adherence to universal rules that govern virtuous behavior, as recognized by the virtuous person (Ames and Rosemont, 2011).

as applied theories of justice, Utilitarianism, Deontology, social contracts, and human rights.[9] It is unclear why—perhaps intuition seems too vague or unquantifiable, or perhaps to Western post-Enlightenment ears, it sounds too much like something that could not be subjected to rigorous analysis and description. In any case, an important takeaway for Rules-First Western mindsets is that Chinese approaches to ethics do not, as a rule, assume that every aspect of ethics can be rigorously analyzed and described.

An example of Awareness also comes from the previous story of Confucius and the two students in *Analects* 11.22. In that case, Awareness consists in Confucius' ability to accurately read the context by perceiving the different temperaments of the two students, inferring how to answer the same question in two different ways for the two different students, and delivering those answers so as to promote desirable outcomes. Another example from the *Analects* is in 3.9, wherein Confucius explains why, in some situations, he goes with tradition against common practice, whereas in other situations, he goes with common practice against tradition. This passage is helpful as it contains an explicit discussion of differing values—maintaining tradition and respect versus frugality—that can compete with and outweigh one another in various ways depending on the specific context.

> 9.3 The Master said, "A ceremonial cap made of linen is prescribed by the rites [禮, effectively a body of guidelines for behavior in a variety of situations, including everyday ones as well as ceremonial and official ones], but these days people use silk. That is frugal, and I follow the majority. To bow before ascending the stairs [when approaching a high-ranking official like a minister or the emperor] is what is prescribed by the rites, but these days people bow after ascending. That is arrogant, and—though it goes against the majority—I continue to bow before ascending."
>
> (Ivanhoe & Van Norden, 2005, p. 25)

Here we see Confucius demonstrating Awareness, not only of how his actions will be perceived by others, but also of the underlying ethical values and

---

9   This is not to be confused with Western ethical "intuitionism," with which there is limited overlap; mostly the two ideas just happen to be associated with the same word.

rationale that would justify different decisions. In one case, ceremonial dress has changed over time. Rather than insist on what is traditional—which one might expect based on stereotypes of many East Asian cultures, stereotypes which sometimes have significant truth behind them—Confucius goes with the general trend of being thriftier, as that is an admirable value that can be accommodated at the same time as showing respect. The rationale for wearing a linen versus silk cap thus involves the interpretation of the guidelines of "ritual propriety," lǐ (禮), according to different contexts and competing considerations (thriftiness and respectfulness). However, in other contexts, e.g., situations where when one bows, Confucius does not go with the general trend which unknowingly exhibits less respect than the more traditional way of bowing. To ascend before bowing implicitly puts the bow-er on the same footing as the bow-ee, for instance a foreign diplomat coming before the emperor. There, respect is the more important underlying value. We see Confucius himself saying what really matters is not a specific rule, but rather understanding different situations. The example, and lǐ itself, combine considerations that, on the face of it, are diverse: tradition, current social norms, thriftiness, ethical values, and even religious values. This is Interconnectedness again, insofar as the varying value-types may in principle be distinguishable, but they are operating in connection with one another in everyday situations (Shun, 2002, p. 53). Furthermore, within Chinese perspectives, the ethically cultivated person—by having Awareness, which means also understanding Context-First—perceives the different types of values operative in any given situation, and understands how to weigh and respect those competing values of different types as much as possible (Yu, Tao, & Ivanhoe, 2009, p. 3).

Another famous example of using Awareness to understand context comes from the Confucian philosopher Mèngzi (孟子), or "Mencius," as he is known in the West. This story is especially interesting in relation to business because there are parallels to guidelines regarding appropriate versus inappropriate touching in the workplace (though the boundaries of appropriateness would be drawn quite differently in the West today).

> 4A17: Chunyu Kun [a rival philosopher] said, "That men and women should not touch in handing something to one another—is this the ritual [as in what is proscribed by lǐ]?"
> Mengzi said, "It is the ritual."

> Chunyu Kun said, "If your sister-in-law were drowning, would you pull her out with your hand?"
>
> Mengzi said, "To not pull your sister-in-law out when she is drowning is to be a beast. That men and women should not touch in handing something to one another is the ritual, but if your sister-in-law is drowning, to pull her out with your hand is discretion."
>
> (Mengzi, 2008, p. 97)

Here, "discretion" is translating the Chinese *quán* (權), which in this sense literally meant weighing things as if on a balance-scale. The takeaway here is that only an uncultivated "beast" would blindly follow normally strict social norms (or rituals of propriety) governing what sorts of touching are appropriate in public. By contrast, the ethically cultivated person understands how such social norms must be weighed against competing values such as compassion and benevolence toward those in need. This is an example of Awareness because what distinguishes the uncultivated "beast" from the cultivated ethical person is discretion or weighing. They appreciate not only the ethically relevant aspects of the situation, but they are also able to weigh competing values (ritual propriety versus compassion and benevolence) and come to the ethical decision. This is also an example of Context-First because context, not rules or such as strict social norms, is primary for guiding ethical behavior.

A final famous and influential example comes from a Daoism-influenced text rather than a Confucian classic. Chapter 8 of *The Art of War* contains a discussion of how to perceive differences in types of terrain and appropriately adapt one's strategy to each.

> And so, a general who thoroughly understands the advantages associated with the nine varieties of terrain knows how to deploy an army. A general who does not thoroughly understand the advantages associated with the nine varieties of terrain will not be able to enjoy what these offer, even though he is familiar with the lay of the land.
>
> (Sunzi, 2011, pp. 51–52)

This passage is a perfect example of Awareness because of the implication that understanding terrain is not the same as (merely) perceiving the lay of the land. The task of the general is distinct from the task of the geographer;

for a general to understand terrain, he or she must understand not just geography, but also how it can promote or inhibit victory against an opponent. This involves more than accurately perceiving the facts at hand (i.e., the lay of the land), and instead having a more penetrating insight into how the facts at hand relate to decision-making. In the case of the general, this means intuiting how to use geography to arrange military resources for victory. In the case of a manager or executive, it means intuiting how to position company resources so as to come out ahead in a negotiation or increase market share, to take just two examples. Terrain-types are thus not "valley," "stream," or "mountain," but rather "difficult," "contested," or "encircling." The terminology may be unfamiliar, but it simply means that the wise decision-maker, whether in combat or business, must understand how the mere facts of any given situation relate to increasing success, whether that be military victory, competitive advantage across a negotiating table, or more ethical decision-making in the (for many Westerners) unfamiliar terrain of China. All that is Awareness, and with that level of understanding, or one might call it insight, one can achieve victory.

The figurativeness of the previous passage is in fact part of its strength—this is a key reason why *The Art of War* is of such enduring fame and relevance not just for strategy in war, but also in politics and business. The person without Awareness sees an obscure passage about generals interpreting the land to win in battle. By contrast, the person with Awareness sees not just the difference between terrain and geography; they also see the underlying wisdom and how it would apply to other situations, for instance in business. According to Chinese perspectives, the ethically cultivated person who can make savvy ethical decisions is not literal-minded and not focused just on the facts. Rather, they perceive the facts and then interpret with Awareness, that trained insight almost like a sixth sense, to see how they can promote more successful decisions—again, whether that's victory in battle, negotiating a better deal, or making more ethical decisions. Gaining Awareness requires first accurately understanding the situations, or contexts, in which one finds oneself, as well as recognizing unexpected interconnections, e.g., between decision-making in military strategy, business strategy, and business ethics. That is why Awareness is on the top of the pyramid in our diagram—to understand it requires understanding Context-First as well as Interconnectedness. Using Awareness to switch from armies and geography to companies and products, we can see how the concept of terrain applies in business.

To demonstrate how understanding and internalizing Chinese perspectives on ethics can help business executives to achieve their business and ethical objectives, we next consider the challenges many Western companies face regarding the protection of intellectual property (IP) in China.

2.4 The legal and moral status of intellectual property rights in China

Companies doing business in and with China face two main types of IP challenges. One involves trademarked and copyrighted physical products. For example, you are manufacturing a branded toy at a factory, and your friend, colleague, or partner observes someone selling knockoffs in a Shanghai market. You don't know exactly how this has happened—it could be an employee who has gone rogue and is trying to make money on the side. Or, it could be that you contracted with a manufacturing firm who then made a second tooling or assembly line and is producing their line of the product in addition to yours. Or, it could be a firm that bought the product legally and then reverse-engineered and mass-produced it. There are further variations on these themes. For example, Chinese firms sometimes produce a product that looks identical, but is not quite of the same quality. Luxury brands like Louis Vuitton and Coach are particularly susceptible to lower-priced "knock-offs" that can look authentic to unsophisticated consumers and "good enough" to savvy shoppers.

Another type of IP challenge in China of special concern to technology companies involves ideas, information, or methods. In the IP realm this could involve patents, trade secrets, or copyrights. For example, an employee may "leak" designs, processes, code, etc. Or, and this is not unique to China, an employee leaves your firm, joins another firm, and suddenly they are producing something that competes with your product yet is very similar to it. A more distinctively Chinese version of this problem arises when a former joint-venture partner, often with a wink and a nod from the government, starts competing with your company with proprietary technology belonging to your company. In one particularly egregious case, an American entrepreneur who entered into a joint venture with a Chinese company to design and manufacture racecars reported that his joint venture partner applied for patents on 510 of his designs without notifying him (Saleen, 2020).

Compounding IP challenges in China is the systematic involvement of the government in technology transfer and its willingness to push the envelope, even as far as state-sponsored corporate espionage (Metha, 2005). In 2020, the chair of Harvard University's Chemistry and Chemical Biology Department and two Chinese nationals were arrested and charged by the US Department of Justice with aiding the Chinese government in stealing intellectual property related to nanotechnology that was created in federally funded labs (Department of Justice, 2020). Later that same year, then-President Trump issued a proclamation "to block certain graduate level and above Chinese nationals associated with entities in China that implement or support China's Military-Civil Fusion (MCF) strategy, from using F or J visas to enter the United States" (The White House, 2020).

IP challenges are illustrative of other property rights issues affecting business, e.g., the enforcement of contracts (Peerenboom, 2002). Property rights, which in most of the rest of the world underpin commercial ventures, are in China weakly protected by the legal system (Chen, 1999). Commercial success and even survival depend on unpredictable and often arbitrary decisions by a murky web of regulators that all trace back eventually to the ruling Communist Party (Peerenboom, 2001, Pei, 2006, Liebman, 2008). What makes the pervasive and serious IP challenges in China so frustrating for Western business executives is that they fly directly in the face of international legal commitments China made to protect the IP of foreign investors in domestic courts when it joined the WTO two decades ago (Clarke, 2003, Hung, 2004). It should be noted that Chinese businesspeople also complain about vague laws, inconsistent enforcement, and the pointlessness of taking legal action (Feldman, 2013, pp. 355, 373). Moreover, as a matter of international law, the United States and the European Union, in support of their companies operating in China, have legal recourse in international fora under Part V of the Trade-related Aspects of Intellectual Property Rights (TRIPS) agreement that gave birth to the WTO in 1995 (World Trade Organization, 1994). In short, since China joined the WTO two decades ago, foreign businesses have had the theoretical right to protect their commercial interests, including IP rights, as a matter of law. In reality, these legal protections are practically non-existent, except when the government wishes to make an example of some person or organization (Yang, 2004, Lam, 2008).

The uncertain and evolving status of property rights in China are a telltale of the degree to which China has made the transition from a state-run economy under authoritarian rule to a market-run economy where the rule of law prevails. At this particular point in time, entering the third decade of the 21st century and the fifth decade of the economic reform era, the transition is far from complete and its ultimate realization is far from assured (Elliot, 2017). Foreign businesses in China thus continue to operate in an informal realm where traditional culture and ethical precepts have considerable enduring influence (Lu & Enderle, 2006, Lu, 2012, Rothlin & McCann, 2016). For Western businesses, this is a bed largely of their own making. In their zeal to remain in the Chinese market and their fear of reprisal from the Chinese government for asserting legal rights, foreign companies and their home countries have for the most part avoided pressing IP and other legal claims in Chinese courts and in international fora. The failure of Western business to promote the rule of law in the first decades of economic reform was a huge missed historical opportunity to influence the path of China's economic and political development. It has impeded transparency and accountability within the Chinese legal system generally, and contributed to a suboptimal environment for foreign investment in China (Santoro, 2009). Thus, while we concede that the property rights interests of foreign business in China would best be served by a strong rule of law enforced by an independent judiciary, the current business environment requires Western business to negotiate IP rights in an environment where traditional culture and ethics continue to hold sway.

In approaching IP protection in China from the standpoint of our Ethical Triad, a threshold issue is the uncertain and evolving status of rights generally, and intellectual property rights in particular. Rights, as they are generally understood today, developed not that long ago in the West. Indeed, whether they were discovered as "natural laws" or merely developed as "positive laws" (or perhaps a mix of both) is a matter for debate in an advanced university seminar on philosophy and the law. What is important for present purposes is that notions of rights as many know them today emerged among Western European philosophers starting approximately four centuries ago. In light of our discussion of Chinese history and culture in Chapter 1, it should come as no surprise that, from Chinese perspectives, rights generally, and the idea of legally protected IP rights in particular, are not only foreign notions but Johnny-come-lately ones to boot. From Chinese perspectives, rights are not a major part of how individuals and organizations interact with one another, or should interact, on a daily basis (Ihara, 2004, pp. 11–30). Higher priorities in China have been and seem to continue to be: social order; economic mobility and economic growth; a sense of being respected as a national power on the world stage; harmony within one's social groups and hierarchies; and, staying out of trouble with the government (Kent, 1993). Hence, appeals to rights, whether they originate from a contractual, constitutional, legislative, or moral basis, just are not recognizable as valid ethical arguments to Chinese mindsets. Moreover, "theft" of intellectual property, in particular, is not viewed as a major offense according to typical Chinese perspectives, as suggested by the title of an important book on the subject: *To Steal a Book is an Elegant Offense: Intellectual Property Law in Chinese Civilization* (Alford, 1995). P. J. Ivanhoe has argued that there are complex and ancient cultural, political, and economic reasons why China was not a fertile ground for the development of robust Western-style notions of IP (Ivanhoe, 2005). This cultural and historical background contributes to the inconsistent, indeed rare, enforcement of IP in the Chinese legal system (Alford, 1995).

Many Chinese businesspeople and political leaders are well aware that developing economies, including European countries and the United States at earlier stages of economic development, tend to have weaker enforcement of IP. In addition, many East Asian economies such as Hong Kong, Taiwan, Singapore, Japan, and South Korea went through processes of IP "violations" as part of their economic growth. Importantly to Chinese perspectives, European and American powers are now pointing fingers, claiming the moral high ground and that they are "in the right" while they themselves were, at earlier stages in their economic development, engaging in the same (or similar) behaviors for which they now publicly criticize and blame Chinese individuals, businesses, and the legal system. Indeed, for some Chinese businesspeople and policymakers, this hypocrisy is thought to effectively give them permission to ignore Western IP claims.[10] A Chinese official, speaking some years in advance of China's entry into the World Trade Organization, explained the historical context of IP in China:

> Intellectual property protection has everything to do with a country's level of development—its resources, science, technology, and

---

10   Some Chinese businesspeople and officials have observed a more retail form of hypocrisy by Europeans and Americans—managers and executives from those very same tech firms, buying knock-offs and counterfeits while visiting China. Consider a particularly poignant account: a Chinese consulate officer whose job it is to protect American industry in this regard observed Polo Ralph Lauren executives buying Polo counterfeits (Feldman, 2013, p. 368).

industry. . . . China's patent law was adopted in 1984, but a patent law in China could not have been imagined before 1979. In those days, knowledge was in the public domain. It would have been wrong to grant a patent. Nowadays, the work of intellectuals is more respected and people realize that creative labor is integral to economic develop-ment. But many people still look at things the old way and believe it is all right to copy others. We must educate people to understand what a patent is and why it is important for science and industry, and we need to encourage inventive activity in our institutions and universi-ties. Without the right attitudes, patent protection has no basis.

(Paine & Santoro, 1995)

It must be admitted that, in addition to explanations based on culture and stages of economic development, the lack of respect for IP ownership is also due, in large measure, to willful, knowing behavior among some Chinese companies and government entities who are quite simply out to get away with as much as they can. At the same time, however, there are significant elements of Chinese culture that help color not only whether IP is a socially valid interest or legal right, but also how one should respond when your IP ownership is disregarded or outright stolen. As we note a number of times in this book, it is possible for two thoughts to be simultaneously true—that China is changing and needs to change in some ways to be part of a global rule-oriented market system, but also that traditional Chinese culture con-tinues to occupy a distinctive role in contemporary Chinese business. We are not suggesting that abandoning legal rights is a wise course for long-term success for investing in and trading with China. Nor should one fail to rec-ognize that there are important forces both in the government and private industry that understand China's future economic development requires a strong IP system that will incentivize scientific discovery and creativity.

We imagine a spectrum, where the extremes are to just give up and go along with Chinese realities relating to rights at one end, and aggressive legal action typified by a "just sue 'em" mentality on the other. If those are the extremes, there are more moderate "middle paths" available, which would, as circumstances require, either engage in dialogue with Chinese partners and government officials or resort to legal remedies in Chinese courts and international tribunals. To be successful, such dialog needs to demonstrate Ethical Awareness, and can be used as an alternative to, or perhaps in tandem with, legal remedies. From a strategic perspective, it makes sense for a business executive intent on securing property rights to keep each potential tactic in reserve to be used according to which gains more practical advantage in the short or long term. Such a strategy is precisely what Master Sun (the same as Sunzi or Sun Tzu) advises in *The Art of War* when he advises leaders to be adaptable:

> the disposition of your [resources] should be like water. Water adapts to the terrain and allows the land to determine its course. An army should adapt to the disposition of enemy forces and allow this to guide them.
>
> (Sunzi, 2011, p. 39)

2.5 Applying the Ethical Triad to protect IP and other commercial rights

Our Ethical Triad suggests two simple proposals for effective protection of IP rights, and indeed all business-related property rights, in China: (i) develop a relationship with your counterpart *prior to* bringing up rights; and (ii) avoid blame, talk in private, emphasize cooperation and collaboration.

First, productive conversations about corporate rights, especially IP-rights, require you to develop a relationship with your counterpart prior to bringing up rights. It can be somewhat difficult to ascertain when a relationship with a counterpart is developed enough for it to be ready for the "rights talk," but a few simple questions can help guide you. Do your counterparts know you as a person—about who you are, your family, interests, and so on? Do you know about your counterparts' families, interests, and so on? If you can have at least somewhat personal conversations, if you have connected as human beings and not just as businesspeople, then you're probably ready to have the rights-talk. In addition to being an application of Context-First (the relationship comes before a rule such as a law) and Awareness (of the cultural-historical-philosophical background of your Chinese counterparts), it is also an application of Interconnectedness. Personal relationships, business relationships, and the networks they comprise are the grounds for motivating more compliant behavior from Chinese counterparts and their businesses.

Second, once you have developed a relationship, you can have the conversation about rights. To be effective and productive, however, such conversations need to avoid blaming and finger-pointing. Both are viewed as highly disrespectful in Chinese culture. To openly accuse someone of doing wrong is a kind of condemnation that is reserved for murderers, rapists, and similarly serious matters. To Chinese mindsets, lying, fraud, and intellectual theft are generally viewed as much less serious than acts like rape, murder, and sedition. For similar reasons, at least initially, conversations about IP need to happen in private, far outside of the public eye. As we have noted, IP rights, and indeed rights generally, are historically foreign to China. As a result, they trigger intense and culturally ingrained resentment at foreign people and powers meddling in Chinese affairs. For many Chinese people, part of what it means to be Chinese is to resist foreign powers imposing their ideas, laws, and economies in China.

Instead of finger-pointing and blaming, conversations about IP rights should instead emphasize the language of cooperation and collaboration. Rather than "this needs to stop" or "you can't do this" or "this is wrong," the language needs to be more like this: "we know a common problem is . . . how can we work together to reduce it" or "this happened . . . how can we collaborate to make sure things go better for both of us in the future?" Conversations will go better if Westerners emphasize mutual benefit, for instance in the form of prestige for both sides, say by having a widely recognized or highly regarded product or process. Typically, what will motivate Chinese counterparts more effectively than overt appeals to rights and legal considerations are appeals to prestige (e.g., for being associated with a successful, recognized product) and mutual advantage. Again, instead of the Western argument "protect this IP because it's mine, I made it" the argument is more like "our having this innovation/product/process, when other people and companies do not, brings prestige to you, to me, and our companies . . . that reputation is to all of our advantage." This kind of language also hints to Chinese counterparts the importance of not letting the Chinese government have access to IP. All this is an application of Awareness regarding what sorts of considerations are more motivating to Chinese mindsets, given the Chinese cultural-philosophical background. Again, we emphasize that the point of learning and applying these principles is not to abandon your IP rights. They are offered as what in many, but not all, instances will be your best chance to actually secure those rights. To illustrate how these ideas can be put into practice, we will draw on two examples, the first of which does not specifically involve IP: Hank Paulson and Goldman Sachs, as well as Bill Gates and the Microsoft Research China (later Asia) team.

Hank Paulson was chairman and CEO of Goldman Sachs, then Secretary of the Treasury during the 2007–2009 crash, and has a long record of successful dealings in China. As a result, he possesses significant Awareness of Chinese perspectives on meeting-protocol, the long process of cultivating and maintaining relationships, and what productive conversations look like. Deals are still done, of course—one way to see the difference is that, to the Western mindset "getting to yes" focuses on the desired end result, the "yes," whereas the Chinese mindset focuses on the journey, the "getting to."

In 1997, Goldman Sachs wanted to handle the privatization, and specifically the initial public offerings (IPOs), of Chinese state-owned telecom companies in the wake of Deng-era economic reforms. Paulson's thought process neatly encapsulates the importance of building a relationship with Chinese Vice Premier Zhu Rongji prior to attempting to do a deal:

> My approach by necessity would have to be a bit circuitous. I wanted to be careful not to presume that any specific deal might be done, or to drag Zhu Rongji too deeply into the details, or worse, to give the impression that I might somehow be asking him to make a decision in favor of us, right then and there.
>
> (Paulson, 2015, p. 6)

Indirectness was also part of Paulson's strategy. This approach was successful, though again success did not look like many Westerners might have expected. As Paulson describes it:

> Then [Zhu] spoke the first of the words we wanted to hear: "Of course, we will consider your opinions, and we hope to cooperate with you. If you are interested in cooperating with the Chinese government in the area of telecommunications, I think you can communicate further with the Ministry of Posts and Telecommunications." That was it, but it was everything.
>
> (Paulson, 2015, p. 12)

Paulson and his team knew that "yes" does not always sound like "yes" in these conversations. He and his team were patient as well as tolerant of this indirectness because they understood that building relationships and negotiating in China are a long game: "As ever, the Chinese [counterparts] had been slow to decide, astonishingly quick to act" (Paulson, 2015, p. 64).

Bill Gates first went to China in 1994 to sell Windows, a product with extremely important IP components. When Gates first traveled to China to promote his product, he had far less experience than Paulson. There were some early bumps in the road—Chinese President Jiang Zemin reportedly said that "Gates should try to understand Chinese language and culture in order to be able to collaborate more" (Buderi & Huang, 2006, p. 1). In our terms, President Jiang was saying that Gates did not yet have sufficient Awareness that Jiang could work with him. Gates learned, however, and over the course of the next ten years took more and longer trips to China. Conversations also became longer, and did not focus on business, but included family, children, poetry, the terra cotta warriors in Xian, and famous Chinese geographical landmarks such as the Three Gorges that span Sichuan and Hubei provinces (Buderi & Huang, 2006, pp. 1–11). In 2004, Harry Shum—then managing director of Microsoft Research China (later Microsoft Research Asia)—was building strong relationships with Chinese academia and education officials. This was in part to secure an intellectual pipeline for Microsoft Research Asia of skilled researchers coming out of Chinese universities. Again, note the indirectness as well as the emphasis on collaboration and building personal relationships: "This meeting is about partnership with academia in Asia. . . . The important thing to the lab is the quality of people" (Buderi & Huang, 2006, p. 21). Helen Meng, an engineering professor at the Chinese University of Hong Kong, explains how this approach was successful: "Microsoft's academic outreach is focused on the long term, which is really smart. . . . Most other companies ask for turnkey solutions but that's not what we're good at" (Buderi & Huang, 2006, p. 22).

Both of these examples illustrate how successful conversations emphasize the benefits each side can offer the other, though it is worth noting that when dealing with the government, the conversations seem to emphasize benefit to China over those to the foreign firm. It is often viewed as a sign of respect to emphasize not just the experience and know-how that your firm brings to the table, but also the potential benefits for Chinese counterparts, firms, and even the government. For example, consider some of the conversations Paulson cites in connection with Chinese telecom IPOs: "this will be a complicated program. . . . But we will spare no effort to provide our skills and specialized knowledge" (Paulson, 2015, p. 13). In reply, Paulson and his team again hear from Zhu Rongji what they want to hear, not "yes" or "agreed," but: "I welcome you to further cooperate with China Construction Bank. By cooperating with your company, CCB will benefit in its commercialization process and speed up its modernization process" (Paulson, 2015, p. 13). In Microsoft's case, the benefits to Chinese individuals, organizations, and society included improving opportunities for Chinese students and engineers to work for prestigious global technology companies and be at the cutting-edge of software and AI research.

2.6 Conclusion: from Ethical Awareness to ethical action

Our advice in this chapter is not just a list of tips and tricks—though some are included. Our Ethical Triad is a holistic approach for Westerners who want to successfully navigate business issues with significant ethical dimensions. It is based on elements of Chinese culture and traditions that date back centuries but still have enormous resonance in contemporary business. As the stories and examples in this chapter have illustrated, Chinese approaches to ethics in general, as well as how ethics relates to business, are fundamentally different from Western approaches. They are based on a unique and complex tradition of etiquette, philosophy, religion, and culture. As daunting as it may seem to master the key elements of this tradition, through our Ethical Triad and through success stories like that of Hank Paulson and Bill Gates, we have attempted to show how every business executive operating in China can successfully negotiate this ethical terrain in business. Our Ethical Triad is what you have to *know*, coming from broadly Western perspectives. However, in ethics as in so many other areas, knowing is not enough: one must *act*. That ability—not just understanding but acting according to the Ethical Triad—we call "Ethical Agility," a topic we shall take up in the next two chapters.

References

Alford, W. (1995). *To steal a book is an elegant offense*. Stanford: Stanford University Press.

Ames, R. T., & Rosemont, H. (2011). Were the early Confucians virtuous? In C. Fraser, D. Robins, & O'Leary, *Ethics in early China: An anthology*. Hong Kong: Hong Kong University Press.

Angle, S., & Slote, M. (2013). *Virtue ethics and Confucianism*. New York: Routledge.

Buderi, R., & Huang, G. (2006). *Guanxi: The art of relationships*. New York: Simon and Schuster.

Chen, J. (1999). *Chinese law: Toward and understanding of Chinese law, its nature and development*. The Hague: Kluwer.

Clarke, D. (2003). China's legal system and the WTO: Prospects for compliance. *Washington University Global Studies Law Review*, 97–118.

Department of Justice: Office of Public Affairs. (2020, January 28). *Harvard University professor and two Chinese nationals charged in three separate China related cases*. Retrieved from www.justice.gov/opa/pr/harvard-university-professor-and-two-chinese-nationals-charged-three-separate-china-related

Elliot, M. (2017, April 17). Why the US can't afford to fall behind in intellectual property enforcement. *Forbes*.

Feldman, S. P. (2013). *Trouble in the middle*. New York: Routledge.

Frankena, W. (1988). *Ethics (Foundations of Philosophy series)* (2nd ed.). New York: Pearson.

Hall, E. T. (1959). *The silent language*. New York: Doubleday.

Hall, E. T. (1977). *Beyond culture*. New York: Anchor Books.

He, B. (2016). A cross-cultural analysis of advertisements from high-context cultures and low-context cultures. *English Language Teaching*, 21–27.

Hung, V. M. Y. (2004). China's WTO commitment on independent judicial review: Impact on legal and political reform. *The American Journal of Comparative Law*, 124.

Ihara, C. (2004). Are individual rights necessary? A Confucian perspective. In K. L. Shun & D. Wong (Eds.), *Confucian ethics* (pp. 11–30). New York: Cambridge University Press.

Ivanhoe, P. J. (2005). Intellectual property and traditional Chinese culture. In J. K. Campbell, M. O'Rourke, & D. Shier (Eds.), *Topics in contemporary philosophy, volume 3: Law and social justice* (pp. 125–142). Cambridge, MA: MIT Press.

Ivanhoe, P. J. (2013). *Confucian reflections: Ancient wisdom for modern times*. New York: Routledge.

Ivanhoe, P. J., & Van Norden, B. W. (2005). *Readings in classical Chinese philosophy* (2nd ed.). Indianapolis: Hackett.

JP Morgan Chase & Co. (2015). *Code of conduct 2019*. Retrieved from www.jpmorgan.com/jpmpdf/1320709777673.pdf

Kent, A. (1993). *Between freedom and subsistence.* Hong Kong: Oxford University Press.

Lam, W. (2008, July 3). The CCP strengthens control over the judiciary. *China Brief, 8*(14).

Liebman, B. L. (2008). China's courts: Restricted reform. *China's Legal System: New Developments, New Challenges,* 620–643.

Lu, X. (2012). *Business ethics: A Chinese approach.* Shanghai: Shanghai Academy of Social Sciences Press.

Lu, X., & Enderle, G. (2006). *Developing business ethics in China.* New York: Palgrave Macmillan.

Lubman, S. (2002). *Bird in a cage: Legal reform in China after Mao.* Stanford: Stanford University Press.

Mengzi. (2008). *Mengzi* (B. W. Norden, Trans.). Indianapolis: Hackett.

Metha, A. (2005). Shifting legal and administrative goalposts: Chinese bureaucracies foreign actors, and the evolution of China's anti-counterfeiting enforcement regime. In N. Diamant, S. Lubman, & K. O'Brien (Eds.), *Engaging the law in China: State, society, and possibilities for justice* (pp. 161–192). Stanford: Stanford University Press.

Nisbett, R. (2003). *The geography of thought: How Asians and Westerners think differently . . . and why.* New York: The Free Press.

Paine, L. S. (1994, March–April). Managing for organizational integrity. *Harvard Business Review, 72.*

Paine, L. S., & Santoro, M. A. (1995). *Pfizer: Global protection of intellectual property.* HBS

No. 9-392-073. Boston, MA: Harvard Business School Publishing.

Paulson, H. (2015). *Dealing with China: An insider unmasks the new economic superpower.* New York: Hachette.

Peerenboom, R. (2001). Globalization, path dependency and the limits of the law: Administrative law reform and the rule of law in the people's republic of China. *Berkeley Journal of International Law, 19.*

Peerenboom, R. (2002). *China's long march toward rule of law.* New York: Cambridge University Press.

Pei, M. (2006). *China's trapped transition: The limits of developmental autocracy.* Cambridge, MA: Harvard University Press.

Pitta, D. A., Fung, H. G., & Isberg, S. (1999). Ethical issues across cultures: Managing the different perspectives of China and the USA. *Journal of Consumer Marketing,* 240–256.

Rosemont, H. (1988). Why take rights seriously? A Confucian critique. In L. Rouner (Ed.), *Human rights and the world's religions* (pp. 167–182). South Bend, IN: Notre Dame University Press.

Rothlin, S., & McCann, D. (2016). *International business ethics: Focus on China.* New York: Springer.

Saleen, S. (2020, July 31). How Chinese officials hijacked my company. *The Wall Street Journal.* Retrieved August 8, 2020, from www.wsj.com/articles/ how-chinese-officials-hijacked-my-company-11596233617

Santoro, M. A. (2009). Chapter 5. In *China 2020: How Western business can— and should—influence social and political change in the coming decade.* Ithaca and London: Cornell University Press.

Sekerka, L. (2009). Organizational ethics education and training: A review of best practices and their application. *International Journal of Training and Development,* 77–95.

Sekerka, L. (2018). Getting ethics training right for leaders and employees. *Wall Street Journal.*

Shun, K. L. (2002). *Ren and Li in the analects* (B. W. Norden, Ed.). New York: Oxford University Press.

Shun, K. L., & Wong, D. (2004). *Confucian ethics: A comparative study of self, autonomy, and community.* New York: Cambridge University Press.

Sunzi. (2011). *The art of war* (P. J. Ivanhoe, Trans.). Indianapolis: Hackett.

Van Norden, B. (2007). *Virtue ethics and consequentialism in early Chinese philosophy.* New York: Cambridge University Press.

Verstappen, S. (2015). *Chinese business etiquette.* Berkeley: Stone Bridge Press.

The White House. (2020, May 29). *President Donald J. Trump is protecting America from China's efforts to steal technology and intellectual property.* Retrieved from www.whitehouse.gov/briefings-statements/president-donald-j-trump-protecting-america-chinas-efforts-steal-technology-intellectual-property/

World Trade Organization. (1994, April 15). *Trade-related aspects of intellectual property rights (unamended version).* From Marrakesh Agreement Establishing the World Trade Organization, Annex 1C, Legal Instruments— Results of the Uruguay Round, 33 I.L.M. 81. Retrieved from www.wto.org/ english/docs_e/legal_e/27-trips_01_e.htm

Yang, D. L. (2004). *Remaking the Chinese Leviathan: Market transition and the politics of governance in China.* Stanford: Stanford University Press.

Yu, K. P., Tao, J., & Ivanhoe, P. J. (2009). *Taking Confucian ethics seriously.* Albany, NY: SUNY Press.

3

CULTIVATING ETHICAL AGILITY

Face and assuring safety and quality in the supply chain

In this chapter, we add the concept of Ethical Agility to our Ethical Triad. The core idea of Ethical Agility is that one must not only understand the ideas of the Ethical Triad, but also be able to put them into action. This requires not just understanding the Triad, but agility in applying it. To accomplish that, i.e., to be ethically agile in China on the most basic level requires fluency with two fundamental elements of Chinese thought, behavior, and culture. These have been at work in several examples we have already considered, but not discussed in explicit detail: "face" which is the English translation of two different words in Chinese, miànzi (面子) or liǎn (臉); and guānxi (關係), which may be loosely translated as influence through reciprocal social connections.

It is safe to say that every Westerner who has ever done business in China has heard of face and guānxi and understands them to be crucial ideas in the Chinese business environment. However, the cultural depths behind these terms are very rarely understood in adequate detail or precision. As a result, face is commonly and over-simplistically thought to involve simply flattery and sensitivity to public image while guānxi is often interpreted as cronyism, or in the worst case, as an opportunity to curry favor through bribery (Santoro, 2009, pp. 101–128). Such superficial and sometimes facile versions of face and guānxi are common, even among executives who have done a considerable amount of business in China. They are, however, misrepresentative of the authentic ethical values and principles behind these familiar terms. These inaccurate interpretations and their sometimes-cynical applications can grease the wheels of commerce in China. They work well enough on some basic level, and they require very little in the way of understanding Chinese culture or personal self-reflection and growth. However, they are very far from maximizing the power of personal-plus-business relationships. With a modicum of study and personal engagement, Western business executives can enjoy a level of cultural interaction with their Chinese counterparts that is both more effective in achieving their commercial and ethical objectives and more personally satisfying in the sense that they can achieve a more authentic experience as world travelers. The latter, we think, is a significant motive for Western businesspeople, the overwhelming majority of whom are, in our experience, in China not only to make money, but also to experience personal growth and to unlock and savor an elusive but intriguing culture. In this and the next chapter, we offer such "reflective practitioners" a more complete and accurate cultural primer on the nuances of these widely heard of, yet rarely understood, keys to unlocking Chinese ethics and effective business relationships. Understanding how to create and maintain guānxi requires understanding face first, so this chapter focuses on face while the next chapter will take up guānxi. We will conclude this chapter by applying what we learn about face to another important and common business ethics and public policy concern—assuring safety and quality in the manufacturing supply chain.

3.1 Ethical Agility: from understanding to action

To develop Ethical Agility is, ethically speaking, to "be water, my friend," as the martial artist Bruce Lee famously put it. This piece of wisdom encapsulates the idea of a mind (and in Lee's case, also a body) that is sufficiently adaptable that it can function effectively in the wide variety of different situations in which it finds itself. As Lee continued: "you put water into a cup, it becomes the cup, you put water into a bottle it become the bottle, you put it into a teapot, it becomes the teapot" (Lee (Li), 1971). This may sound quite figurative, but the point is straightforward: water, by its very nature, adapts its shape to fit the contours of the vessel. The vessel is a metaphor for concrete situations in which one finds oneself. For the martial artist, "situations" might mean primarily fights, whereas for the businessperson doing business in a global environment, it means adaptability in making and carrying out decisions with ethical implications. Though this is a general observation—familiar to businesspeople with experience in many parts of the world—we focus on the adaptability required to conduct ethical business in China, and hence as informed by our Ethical Triad.

Ethical Agility involves internalizing the Ethical Triad—Context, Interconnectedness, and Awareness—to the point of being able to put this mode of thinking into practice: to turn understanding into behavior, to turn knowing *that* into knowing *how*. For Westerners, we anticipate that this will be an adjustment, especially at first, because we are talking about internalizing a fundamentally different way of thinking about ethics to the point where one can put it into practice. The flexibility required by Ethical Agility may seem intimidating or just overly philosophical, but an obvious point should be encouraging: over a billion Chinese people practice Ethical Agility every day!

As we have emphasized throughout this book, by introducing the concept of Ethical Agility and advocating fluency in more than one moral language, we are not advocating anything as coarse as "when in China do whatever the Chinese do." Nor are we advocating abandonment of one's antecedent ethical frameworks and business objectives. One can gain skills—in this case ethical ones—without losing others, for example, cross-training in different sports, learning multiple languages, or adapting to different corporate cultures as one moves from or interacts with different employers or clients. Consider the famous adage (widely misattributed to Aristotle) that it is the mark of an educated mind to be able to entertain a thought without necessarily accepting it. The educated, or as we would put it, "ethically agile" person can appreciate other modes of thought and behavior without necessarily giving up their own antecedent moral values and business objectives, just as one can learn to speak French without forgetting how to speak English.

We can begin to appreciate what it means to practice Ethical Agility by revisiting the all-too-common story of The Hurried Executive from the previous chapter. The Hurried Executive, the reader will recall, flew into China with the unrealistic expectation that a few days would be sufficient to secure a lucrative contract. How could The Hurried Executive have done better? The first step, perhaps outside the immediate control of the executive, was for their superiors to be better-informed, thereby realizing that three days in China is utterly insufficient for making first contact and getting to the point of signing an advantageous contract. The better strategy would have followed a completely different script. First, knowing that there is no real separation between what is business and what is personal (Interconnectedness), the executive could have started by building personal relationships with the people they wanted to do business with. That would have involved committing more time to the trip, practicing some basic pleasantries in Mandarin as well as some basic Chinese manners, bringing (Foreign Corrupt Practices Act-acceptable) gifts for their contacts with a nicer but still-legal one for the most senior contact, and being ready to converse on basic social topics such as family, travel, geography, music, art, and food. With a little study and consideration, they could have added more specialized topics such as Chinese scroll painting, and, of course, varieties of tea! It is important, under these circumstances, to be willing and able to open up about one's life and family, so that the Chinese partners perceive that the executive's intentions are genuine, but also feel comfortable that they are actually getting to know the person. Much of this may seem like it is not "real ethics" or "real business" but, as we have noted, because of Interconnectedness, there are no sharp divisions between what is business and what is personal, and what is mere etiquette and what is ethics. Understanding Interconnectedness, and being able to put it into practice via Ethical Agility, the savvy executive would avoid the mistakes of The Hurried Executive, thereby opening the door to a much more productive and financially rewarding relationship with the Chinese managers.

Some Westerners might regard the process of acquiring Ethical Agility we describe as too demanding, time-consuming, and expensive. In Chinese terms, they have "drawn the line." A classic cultural reference for this concept comes, unsurprisingly, from The Master himself (Confucius) in *The Analects*, during a conversation with one of his students, Ran Qiu.

6.12 Ran Qiu said, "It is not that I do not delight in your Way, Master, it is simply that my strength is insufficient."

The Master said, "Someone whose strength is genuinely insufficient collapses somewhere along the Way. As for you, you deliberately draw the line."

(Ivanhoe & Van Norden, 2005, pp. 17–18)

Here, the "Way" refers to a way of living that Confucius advocated, which became both a philosophy and a religion, and was a founding influence on Chinese culture. That influence has endured; to this day, the Confucian way of life is a central and common component of distinctively Chinese ways of life, including in business and ethics. According to historical accounts, Confucius embodied his way to an extraordinary degree. For him, one should cultivate certain virtues—some of which we will discuss in Chapter 5—and that in doing so, one lives a better and more harmonious life. Ran Qiu, the student, claims he finds this Way too difficult, and Confucius calls him out for instead having implicitly decided that he is unable, rather than first putting in a real effort. Western executives who remain glued to the view that learning about Chinese culture and building personal relationships with their counterparts are too inscrutable, complex, time consuming, or costly have "drawn the line." They have, whether they know it or not, already decided that the Way (or perhaps more accurately the Ways) of doing business in China are too difficult. We believe this can be boiled down to a clear, if sometimes hard, choice: are companies and individuals willing to invest sufficient time and effort in the "soft stuff" we describe in order to take advantage of the commercial opportunities in China, as well as to honor their values and fulfill their ethical commitments?

Thus far we have emphasized the differences between our framework and typically Western frameworks, but the idea of Ethical Agility should not seem totally foreign. An important idea within both Eastern and Western approaches to ethics, beginning in ancient times, is that one grows into being an ethical person by practicing ethically correct thought and behavior until it becomes almost second nature. Confucius, as well as his followers Mencius (Mèngzi, 孟子) and Xúnzi (荀子), would have agreed with Aristotle on this point (Ivanhoe & Van Norden, 2005, p. 5, Mèngzi, 2008, pp. xxiii–xxxvii, Xúnzi, 1994, pp. 139–168). As with other skills—such as martial arts, driving or cooking, as well as skills associated with games and sports—you can, with practice and attention toward improving, get to a point where you no longer have to think consciously about what you are doing. We are all, at some level, familiar with this process, whether it be skills as relatively simple as tying shoes or using chopsticks, riding a bike, ironing clothes, dribbling a basketball, or driving. Aristotle argued explicitly, in fact, that ethical thought and behavior are skills not that different from others (Aristotle, 2012), another point on which he could have agreed with Confucians as well as Daoists. An important point worth re-emphasizing is that one is not limited to only a single skill. In the same way that one can be skilled at several games, sports, or martial arts, one can be skilled in several ways—or Ways—of ethical thought and behavior. The idea of Ethical Agility means adopting an additional framework for thinking about and doing ethics.

3.2 *Miànzi* and *liǎn*: moving beyond overly-simplified notions of face in Chinese ethics to achieve insider status

To have Ethical Agility one must participate appropriately in both face and guānxi. To become fluent in guānxi, however, one must first become fluent in face, so we consider face first. The English word "face" is the translation for two distinct but related Chinese concepts of how one shows and receives respect. Each concept has its own word in Chinese, but they are both commonly translated as "face" into English. As a first approximation, we can think of one form of face—liǎn (臉)—as being more inward-focused, while the other more outward-focused form is called miànzi (面子). The latter is easier for Westerners to comprehend and engage with, but we caution that it is only part of the idea of face. For one to have face in terms of miànzi means that other people outwardly treat one as having prestige, social status through influence and connections, as well as personal, professional, and financial success. There is a kind of symbiosis here; the more of those things one actually has, the more face one expects to be shown but simultaneously the more that other people render outward shows of respect, the more face (miànzi) one has. Liǎn is more inward-directed in the sense that it is less about how much respect other people show, and is instead about whether a person is perceived as having an upstanding moral character and is thought to exhibit decent behavior under all circumstances (Hu, 1944). If one has significant liǎn, it is believed that they should be conferred significant miànzi as well, insofar as to typical Chinese mindsets one deserves or warrants success and prestige (miànzi) if one is perceived as having good character (liǎn).

Both forms of face are important for doing business in Chinese culture contexts. However, miànzi, the outward-directed form, is more important for Westerners because they can take actions to increase miànzi for their Chinese counterparts and thereby gain greater opportunities, cooperation, and compliance. Even though there is less that Western executives can do to promote liǎn for their Chinese counterparts, as part of having Awareness, they should know that liǎn is operating just below the surface.

Miànzi and liǎn interact in complex ways. For example, in part because of the importance of appearances, one does not necessarily need liǎn to contribute to another person's miànzi. For instance, if an executive's subordinates consistently show them exceptionally high levels of respect, they will as a result have considerable miànzi among that group and at the company in general, even if not every single one of their subordinates are considered the very most upstanding individuals (i.e., not every one of them has great liǎn). However, in general, upstanding individuals (those with considerable liǎn) can promote miànzi to a greater degree because those are the individuals whose opinions matter most. In time, a Westerner can acquire liǎn such that their rendering of face to their Chinese counterpart will be more meaningful. But building up such social capital is something that takes time and experience in the culture. It is in a sense the ultimate sign that one has been successful in acquiring Ethical Agility.

Westerners with an inadequate understanding of what face is and how to confer it on a Chinese host are as likely to unwittingly blunder away opportunities as they are to solidify a business relationship. Examples abound. Recall from Chapter 1 the story of the American agricultural company that wanted to secure an agreement to conduct field tests for their pesticide on a Chinese state farm. The company brought boxes of hats emblazoned with the company's name and its trademark color—green. For their Chinese counterparts, to put on green hats would be for them to have made themselves look foolish, given that wearing a green hat is commonly thought to signify in traditional Chinese culture that your wife or girlfriend is cheating on you. The association with infidelity dates back to the Yuan Dynasty (1279–1368) when the relatives of prostitutes were forced to wear green hats. In Chinese the phrase itself, "to wear a green hat (dài lù mào zǐ, 戴綠帽子)," sounds similar to a word for a cuckold. As soon as company officials handed out the green hats, expecting their Chinese counterparts to put them on, the Westerners had publicly revealed themselves as clueless of the fact that it would cause a loss of face. This cluelessness meant that the Westerners, aside from already being foreigners, were also outsiders in the sense of not being "in the know" about salient Chinese culture. Cultural gaffes such as the green hat example are not completely avoidable, especially by foreigners and even in many cases by foreign-born Chinese. A common trope in movies about Chinese families and relationships concerns how Western-born Chinese people, though they often know more about the cultural environment than many Westerners, still get "little" things like greetings and titles wrong. This becomes a source of criticism and negative judgments from Chinese, Taiwanese, or Singapore-born Chinese folks, even to the tune of shaming or shunning a significant other, or as one reason (often among many) to oppose an engagement.[11] Because of Interconnectedness, ethics, etiquette, and culture are not sharply distinguished. Nor are formal versus informal occasions—Chinese businesspeople often use informal as well as formal gatherings to gauge Westerners in terms of sincerity, personality, cultural fluency, and dependability (Pye 1992, Hu, Grove, & Enping 2010, Chapters 6 & 8). As a result, "little" things are not so little.

Though generally perfection is not expected from Westerners, a fairly high degree of cultural fluency—Ethical Agility—is required for participating properly in conferring or diminishing face. Mistakes as seemingly minor as handing out green hats can be perceived by Chinese mindsets as serious losses of face, and depending on severity are thought of as giving Chinese folks permission to dismiss or in other ways take Westerners less seriously (ethically speaking). Western businesspeople start with the automatic demerit of being a foreigner, and must overcome that demerit by demonstrating successful practice of face (and guānxi). Our claim is not the unreasonable expectation that Westerners must get face and guānxi perfect in order to overcome the demerit. Nor do we defend the demerit system per se. But the stakes of getting these basic ideas right are real (Pye 1992, De Menthe, 2013, Feldman, 2013, Verstappen, 2015, Wenzhong, Grove, & Euping, 2010). To succeed in business in China one must gain the ability to demonstrate that one appreciates the force of face and guānxi, even if one does not get them right perfectly or all the time. At stake is whether your Chinese hosts will view you as a potential insider whom they can trust and do business with, or a barbarian outsider that can, at best, be worked with at arm's length.

The insider-outsider distinction helps explain one of the oft-cited paradoxes about China and other parts of East Asia that have been influenced by some of the same cultural sources as China. The apparent paradox involves

---

11   For example, see the character Billi in *The Farewell* over several conversations with her parents and eventually one with her whole family over a meal (Wang, 2019). Or, see Rachel in the scene where she makes *jiǎozi* with the Young family in *Crazy Rich Asians* (Chu, 2018).

the widespread practice of keeping one's distance, not shaking hands, and waiting for superiors to speak (e.g., during introductions and meetings), in contrast with the chaotic and uncomfortable "every person for themselves" environment of subways and other public transit where people shove, jostle, and bump one another. How can a culture that insists on such highly ritualized respectful behavior in business meetings tolerate such disorganized and disrespectful chaos in public spaces? Aside from the practical challenge of millions of people needing to get to work, the answer is that, in public, almost everyone is a stranger—an outsider who does not demand the same level of expressions of respect. By contrast, in business, because there is no separation between what is business and personal, achieving some measure of insider status is very important.

3.3 Face and Facebook: Mark Zuckerberg misplays the name game

Some gaffes are more serious than the green hats story and can mark you as a barbarian outsider. When Mark Zuckerberg asked President Xi to name his soon-to-be-born first child it was a clumsy attempt at cultural interaction that turned into an embarrassing setback. Mr. Zuckerberg had spent a year studying Mandarin. He had recommended Xi's book *The Governance of China* (Xi, 2015) to Facebook employees. His wife, the pediatrician and philanthropist Priscilla Chan, was of Chinese ancestry and grew up speaking Cantonese. So, when he cornered Xi at a state dinner at the White House and asked him to name his unborn daughter, he must have been feeling pretty good about his chances.

It would seem, at first glance, hard to fault Mr. Zuckerberg for earnestness or effort. Yet he managed to appear foolish and at the same time make President Xi feel uncomfortable by having to fend him off. What went wrong between Mr. Zuckerberg and President Xi? It is difficult to know where to start because there are so many aspects of his awkward entreaty worth pondering. A threshold point apparently lost on Zuckerberg is that, typically, business leaders do not have the same social standing or prestige in China as they do in some parts of the West and especially the United States. Historically, being a businessperson was considered lower in status than being a scholar or government minister, for example, let alone an emperor or chairman of the Party. As a result, President Xi very probably sees himself on the same plane as the presidents, prime ministers, kings, and queens of major world powers. The leader of a business, even one as valuable and famous as Facebook, is, to Chinese perspectives, decisively outranked by such a senior Chinese leader. In short, Mr. Zuckerberg, who would be a much sought-after star at any American dinner party, was severely outclassed and did not grasp how socially presumptuous he must have seemed to Xi.

A second obvious point is that President Xi well understood that Facebook had been aggressively trying (unsuccessfully) to enter the Chinese market for years and he must have felt that the naming request was a rather blunt and unsubtle way of advancing Mr. Zuckerberg's real, i.e., business, purpose. Xi must also have perceived, with some justification, that Mr. Zuckerberg and Facebook, whether intentionally or unintentionally, would present a challenge to Chinese culture and society, and to the ruling Communist Party (Mozur, Scott, & Isaac, 2017). Xi is well aware that Facebook and other Western social media platforms like Twitter have been instrumental parts of revolutionary activity in other parts of the world, and hence would be anathema to Chinese government leaders' desire for stability and control (Pye, 1988). President Xi knows that it is easier to control Chinese social media platforms which are functionally as good or better than Facebook. Under the circumstances, Mr. Zuckerberg's request would have been perceived by Xi as wildly underestimating his intelligence and grasp of the terrain over which Facebook hoped to operate in China.

Most importantly, however, Mark Zuckerberg did not have the right kind of relationship with President Xi. The naming of a child, especially a first-born, is something that is appropriate to ask of an elder relative like a favorite aunt or uncle. It is a special honor that rests on a preexisting and close personal relationship. It was highly presumptuous of Mr. Zuckerberg to make such a request of a person who not only outranked him, but was also someone to whom he was an outsider and had perhaps met once or just a few times. Assuming that learning a little Mandarin would be a sufficient personal bond with Xi highlighted a lack of cultural Awareness. All these considerations taken together gave President Xi permission to dismiss Zuckerberg's request, humiliating him by an outright rejection, rather than, for example, letting him down easily. (We hasten to add that despite this one significant setback, all is not necessarily lost permanently for Mr. Zuckerberg. He has virtually unlimited resources and access, if he seeks it, to knowledgeable China hands who can help him learn how to operate in China the way

Hank Paulson and his tech counterpart Bill Gates before him learned to do. The Mandarin lessons may yet pay off.)

Mark Zuckerberg's high-stakes bid to confer face and smooth Facebook's business path in China resulted instead in his own personal loss of face in a highly public way. More significant than any personal humiliation Zuckerberg suffered is the fact that by behaving so cluelessly, he marked himself as an outsider barbarian—someone who could not be trusted and who makes a poor prospect for a business relationship. It takes Awareness: a reading of the specific situation and the relationships involved to discern how to properly and effectively promote face. Mr. Zuckerberg failed to understand the importance of hierarchies and closeness of relationships. This is such a complex and central aspect of Chinese ethics, etiquette, culture, religion, and philosophy that we devote the entire next chapter to it. It was a great honor for Mr. Zuckerberg to even meet President Xi, not an opportunity for him to ask a significant personal favor. Mr. Zuckerberg did not have the type of longstanding, preexisting, and personal relationship that would constitute permission for such an ask.

Beyond understanding hierarchies and relationships, another simple but crucial principle to grasp, in order to properly and effectively confer face, is that Chinese businesspeople often see themselves as hosts to Western business executives. Western businesspeople who think of themselves as guests, and of their Chinese contacts as hosts, will have a much smoother time doing business in China (Buderi & Huang, 2006, Hu et al. 2010, De Menthe, 2013, Collinsworth, 2014). Understanding this host-guest dynamic, a savvy executive will be prepared with questions calculated to give the host opportunities to show what they know. By asking informed questions and then really listening to replies, the Westerner can effectively confer face upon their host. As one longtime traveler to China put it:

> [W]esterners need to understand that *respect* is much more than a matter of not violating another's rights; it also includes showing interest in and appreciation of their *distinctive* way of life. . . . That is to say, it includes things that are about peoples and not just persons.
>
> (Ivanhoe, Interview, 2020)

The Westerner who is able to achieve Ethical Agility by understanding hierarchies and relationships and by understanding their own role and context as guests, will be savvier in conferring face effectively to their hosts. The rewards of such Ethical Agility are great, as they could potentially result in the ultimate influence that comes with being thought of an insider rather than an outsider. To better understand how to put the ideas we have been discussing about Ethical Agility and face into practice, we now turn to a real-world example. A common issue Westerners encounter when doing business in China is maintaining quality and safety in the manufacturing supply chain. In the next section, we focus specifically on safety and efficacy in the chemical and pharmaceutical outsourcing sector, but the principles we describe about how to employ Ethical Agility to help assure the safety and quality of finished products and intermediate ingredients and components are more broadly applicable to other kinds of supply chains.

3.4 Safety and efficacy failures in a pharmaceutical supply chain: the heparin tragedy of 2008

The Chinese supply chain value proposition is a familiar one. In order to pare expenses and be more competitive, American and European companies buy ingredients for prescription and over-the-counter drugs from companies in China. These include active pharmaceutical ingredients (APIs), as well as other components and delivery mechanisms that make up a wide array of pharmaceutical therapies. Supply chains are often long, labyrinthine, and lack transparency. It is a major challenge for companies and regulators alike to figure out exactly where everything comes from that winds up in a given drug sold in the West, and whether each component has been manufactured under Good Manufacturing Practices (GMP), the high standard that governs drugs distributed in the United States and Europe even when manufactured elsewhere.

A particularly alarming example of what can go wrong in a pharmaceutical supply chain was the heparin recall of 2008. Just after the New Year, two children undergoing dialysis at St. Louis Children's Hospital experienced severe allergic reactions. Their eyelids swelled, heartbeats quickened, and blood pressure dropped within two minutes of being hooked up to dialysis machines for their regular treatments. The attending physicians at the hospital had seen similar reactions a few weeks earlier. At the time, the doctors assumed it was a problem with the sterilization of the dialysis equipment. When the second incidents occurred, Dr. Alexis M. Edward realized "we really need to report this" (Rockoff, 2008).

After learning about Dr. Edward's findings, the US Centers for Disease Control and Prevention (CDC) posted internet notices and advisories about the unusual adverse reactions. Within two days, the CDC received reports of similar reactions among 50 adult dialysis patients in six states. The cause of the allergic reactions turned out to be contamination in the blood thinner heparin which was used in dialysis as well as in treating heart attack victims and in heart surgery. By April 2008 the CDC counted over 700 reports of serious side effects among heparin users and perhaps as many as 62 deaths attributable to contaminated heparin (Gibson & Singh, 2018). The manufacturer, Baxter International, Inc., recalled heparin products in the US as did companies in Canada, Japan, Italy, Denmark, and Germany (Kelly, 2008).

Eventually, the supply chain led back to a contaminated ingredient manufactured in China. Baxter bought the pharmaceutical ingredient from a Milwaukee, Wisconsin-based firm, Scientific Protein Laboratories, then owned by a Bethesda, Maryland-based leveraged buyout firm called American Strategies. Scientific Protein Labs made the contaminated ingredient at a plant it co-owned with a local Chinese company, Changzhou SPL. It turned out that the Changzhou plant manufacturing the contaminated ingredient and exporting it to the United States was not even registered as a drug manufacturer with the Chinese regulatory authorities, and so had never been examined by either US or Chinese authorities. The supply chain for the adulterated product reached even deeper into manufacturing facilities far from either Chinese, European, or US government regulation. Changzhou purchased the adulterated heparin from two wholesalers who in turn gathered the raw materials from smaller producers, many of which were family operations.

When the FDA started investigating in February 2008, it found that the active ingredients from Changzhou were contaminated with a cheap, unapproved ingredient—over-sulphated chondroitin sulfate (OSCS)—modified to mimic heparin. OSCS is not ordinarily found in nature. Normally, heparin is made from pig intestines, which were often handled and processed by many smaller operations, who then sold the product to middlemen, who in turn sold it to Chinese companies like Changzhou SPL (Gibson & Singh, 2018, pp. 24–26). OSCS, on the other hand, is created through chemical synthesis of chondroitin sulphate, which is derived from animal cartilage. Scientific Protein claimed that the contaminant was already in the crude heparin by the time it found its way to Changzhou. Because OSCS mimics heparin, it cannot be detected by routine quality control testing. The FDA found that anywhere from 2 to 50 percent of the suspect heparin samples consisted of OSCS. The introduction of a cheap, chemically synthesized contaminant designed to mimic heparin and evade detection suggests the troubling likelihood that the contamination was intentional rather than accidental. Further support for this possibility comes from the fact that pig prices had risen dramatically because of an outbreak of blue-ear disease affecting pigs in China starting in 2006, making the financial incentive to cheat even stronger (Gibson & Singh, 2018, p. 25). Thanks to the vigilance of the doctors at St. Louis Children's Hospital and the quick response of the CDC and other authorities, the potential harm of the heparin contamination was limited to 62 deaths. However, the heparin incident could have been even more tragic if public health safety alert systems had not caught the problem.

The heparin case exemplifies how things can go very wrong in a supply chain. Effective management of safety and quality in a supply chain requires a more proactive approach which, among other things, identifies potential issues, organizes manufacturing processes and policies to avert defects, and establishes an effective plan of remediation. Drug manufacturing in particular is a highly regulated area. In addition to regulation by Chinese authorities, the US Food and Drug Administration has several field offices in China to help assure that manufacturers follow GMP. The European Medicines Agency has held high-level regulatory harmonization meetings with their Chinese counterparts. These regulatory frameworks are, however, inadequate to oversee the multitude of facilities in drug supply chains originating in China. Despite such imperfect intergovernmental regulatory efforts, ultimately the responsibility to assure the safety and efficacy of the supply chain rests with the company at the top of the supply chain that will distribute the product to doctors and patients. How then can Ethical Agility and an understanding of the concept of face help executives to manage safety and efficacy in their supply chains?

3.5 Getting to "we": agility and the role of face in preventing supply chain problems from boiling over into supply chain disasters

A hypothetical based on the facts of the heparin case provides an apt illustration of how to be Ethically Agile and effectively manage supply chain safety and efficacy. Let us imagine that, *before any patients were harmed,*

Baxter and Scientific Protein became aware of, or even just suspected, quality control issues at Changzhou SPL. When they investigate, they discover that Changzhou was sourcing ingredients from middlemen, who in turn buy ingredients from small independent producers, which are often family-run operations. Those operations are supposed to be working with pig entrails to produce raw ingredients for heparin, but in some cases, are substituting OSCS to cut costs, presumably as a result of the higher price of pigs following the outbreak of blue-ear disease two years earlier.

Clearly the imperative is to fix the supply chain problem—quickly and verifiably. How best to do this? The Western mindset on these kinds of issues is pretty set. Someone from the "home office" shows up to ask a lot of questions and impose order and discipline on the process. It is not necessary to consider the ethical perspectives and cultural sensitivities of Changzhou executives. Perhaps that is even perceived as a distraction or pandering. Chinese manufacturers expect to be a part of, and profit from, the global trading system and so they should be expected to conform to global safety and efficacy standards. Full stop. No need to consider local cultural niceties and sensitivities. Everyone in the supply chain needs to snap to it. As we have noted previously, this perspective has a lot of merit behind it. The only question is whether it is the most effective way to accomplish the most important goal—to assure the safety and efficacy of the drug supply chain and avoid seriously injuring or killing patients.

Consider, however, the perspective of the Changzhou managers: a bunch of foreigners with little local authority, whom you have never seen before, are flinging accusations at you, causing you to lose face. A common reaction under these circumstances would be to not only limit access to the plant, but slow the inspection process down while appearing outwardly polite and compliant. It is also common to claim that slowdowns, or even limited access itself, are caused by mysterious company policies, state or company bureaucracy, absent managers or employees, or recent illnesses. Miscommunications may also be blamed. Overt stonewalling is typically avoided as it is considered rude to Chinese perspectives, but excuses and half-explanations for delays and lack of access are either real and exaggerated, or invented from whole cloth. Frustrated, and nearly as befogged as before, the Baxter and Scientific Protein teams are unable to achieve real clarity on what happened at Changzhou SPL. Far too often, the situation descends into an international merry-go-round of counterproductive finger-pointing (Gibson & Singh, 2018, p. 26).

A better way for Westerners to approach such a difficult conversation, one that would confer appropriate face on the Chinese counterparts and would better accomplish their goal of making safe and effective products, would be with a script like this:

> We are having some trouble with the heparin supply in the US and Europe. We found this batch of heparin that contains a chemical compound which has replaced some of the compound derived from pig entrails. We are hoping we can collaborate with you—with your experience and expertise, we are hoping to figure out where the altered heparin came from. That way, we can help our customers and patients and stop them from getting hurt.

This approach avoids common affronts to face that Westerners commit unawares, by: acknowledging the intelligence and ability of the Chinese manager; in that light asking for help; avoiding anything that sounds like an accusation or assigning blame; adopting a cooperative problem-solving attitude, and finally; giving the manager the option to agree to help. This last is especially important because it offers Chinese managers opportunities to help "save the day" by uncovering problems in the supply chain. A further benefit is that those same managers and their coworkers are likely to be more vigilant on your behalf in achieving compliance by middlemen and producers further down the supply chain.

An important feature of scripts like these is that they offer the manager a way forward by preserving their face. By not assuming fault or responsibility on the part of the representatives of the Chinese firm, in fact implicitly assuming that the problem lies elsewhere, one not only avoids insulting the Chinese manager but simultaneously allows them the opportunity to either find blame and responsibility elsewhere, or to eventually acknowledge some of the responsibility on behalf of the Chinese firm, or a mix of both (as the facts on the ground require). One way to promote your own Ethical Agility in situations like these is to focus on addressing the problem, which is after all a "we"-problem in the sense that the foreign managers need the cooperation of the Chinese firm's managers, while setting aside outward assignments of responsibility and blame. All of this is part of Ethical Agility, being able to apply one's understanding—Awareness—of what counts as respectful and disrespectful in Chinese contexts so as to protect and even promote face.

A related and common mistake occurs when Westerners arrive at the Chinese firm equipped with failed test results, a list of demands, and an overt expectation to uncover wrongdoing (if not outright accusations). As with making plans for a site visit, a much more effective approach is to treat representatives of the Chinese firm with what they will recognize as respect. That is, to treat them as valued collaborators rather than as wrongdoers, or even suspected wrongdoers. The better approach would include references to the following sorts of issues: the grave risk to their firm and yours because of tragic deaths and media coverage; the resulting harm to reputations as well as the relationship your firm has with theirs; your firm's direct obligations to the patients who might suffer and die if the problem is not fixed; how that necessitates the need for a speedy outcome; and the grave embarrassment as well as expense when regulators, especially foreign regulators, show up.

Another common mistake is to be outwardly in a hurry, demanding meetings and access right away. Again, a better approach is to acknowledge that the managers of the Chinese firm must be very busy and have important work to do, but to ask them to sit down to dinner or tea so that the matter can be discussed. In reality of course, this should have been planned when the visit was arranged; as a show of respect, they should have asked if it would be polite to offer to take representatives of the Chinese firm out to dinner. In a pinch, tea or coffee together with the associated connotations of a more social environment could suffice, as it expresses the hope that both sides will sit down like civilized collaborators. In Chinese culture contexts, it is expected that a problem, including its immediacy and its size, will be discussed in some detail before any requests are made for help. This should be viewed by Western businesspeople as an opportunity to indirectly but clearly reveal (rather than bluntly assert) how dire the situation is, or could easily become. Demands for information, help, and other things are *verboten*: demands are reserved for how parents treat children; schoolmasters treat students (especially those that misbehave); and for how powerful, inconsistent, and distant Chinese government officials address problematic citizens and organizations, usually to make examples out of them. Awareness of Chinese contexts and mindsets is needed to realize how profoundly rude making demands would be, to Chinese counterparts.

As explained previously, outwardly hurried and adversarial behavior from Westerners renders them clueless buffoons, thereby giving Chinese businesspeople implicit permission to treat Western counterparts (and even their companies) as outsiders and hence ethically undeserving, i.e., dismissively. At that point, Western counterparts become people to say yes and nod to, to misdirect endlessly, and to get rid of as quickly as possible. Again, as far as representatives from the Chinese firm are concerned, foreign executives are presumed guests in China and of the Chinese firm. As a result, the Chinese expectation is that Westerners will act like guests, where coming in hot is rude to the point of being unethical in Chinese culture contexts, displaying a lack of respect, and resulting in a corresponding erosion of face. Such uncouth behavior underscores ancient and widespread Chinese preconceptions that foreigners really are just barbarians that never learn. Once managers from each company have had a chance to sit down and get acquainted, the matter of impure heparin can be broached.

We acknowledge that the approach we have outlined may seem counterintuitive or even circuitous to Western executives. "We are talking about drug safety," one may understandably argue; "how can the situation demand that we do anything but go in and be very direct and to the point to solve a critical problem?" It seems viscerally inappropriate to react to a quality and safety issue with anything less than righteous indignation and hot pursuit. While we understand and appreciate the concerns behind such sentiments, our answer to this question is quite simple. What would you rather do—express your righteous indignation and elevated concern, or solve the problem? If you want to solve the problem, and if it's in China, our approach is much more likely to be successful. The approach we have outlined is no less concerned about drug safety and efficacy than is the Western "home office" approach. Understanding and applying the concepts of face can help executives to manage their supply chains so that problems don't boil over into disasters.

Another objection to the practice of Ethical Agility is that it is not compatible with the way supply chain compliance is usually done, i.e., with a comprehensive checklist of concerns that (often independent) auditors test and validate. Our reply to this objection is two-fold. First, what we are describing is the best way to remediate a problem once it has been identified. This is compatible with a compliance mindset. Ethical Agility is a skill that can help you fix a problem, but companies still need compliance systems and protocols to exercise proper oversight in a supply chain. A second point we would make is that Ethical Agility is a valuable skill to have in the design of compliance systems. One size does not fit all. Things are less like to go wrong in the first place if compliance systems incorporate what, from a cultural perspective, is likely to work or not work in a particular place. In China, that means exercising Ethical Agility and being able to put into practice knowledge of traditional Chinese culture.

3.6 Conclusion: face and *guānxi*

The point of being able to properly show and receive respect according to Chinese custom—being fluent in face—is to make a transition from an outsider to an insider who can unlock the power of relationships and networks. With such relationships and networks comes increased access, faster responses, and overall, far greater cooperation. Such connections, when coupled with more vigilant supervision of the facts on the ground, could have prevented the heparin tragedy. In short, practicing Ethical Agility would have given Baxter a better chance of knowing what was happening on the ground sooner so that it could be corrected, and, in the worst case, they could have facilitated faster, more efficient responses once the crisis developed. In the next chapter we will explore the topic of Ethical Agility in greater depth by taking up a concept closely related to face—*guānxi*—an idea much invoked by Westerners, but which, like face, is often very poorly understood and put into practice.

References

Aristotle. (2012). *Nichomachean ethics* (R. Bartlett & S. Collins, Eds. & Trans.). Chicago: University of Chicago Press.

Buderi, R., & Huang, G. (2006). *Guanxi: The art of relationships*. New York: Simon and Schuster.

Chu, J. M. (Director). (2018). *Crazy rich Asians* [Motion Picture]. Los Angeles: Warner Bros. Pictures.

Collinsworth, E. (2014). *I stand corrected*. New York: Doubleday.

De Menthe, B. L. (2013). *The Chinese way in business*. North Clarendon, VT: Tuttle.

Feldman, S. P. (2013). *Trouble in the middle*. New York: Routledge.

Gibson, R., & Singh, J. P. (2018). *China Rx*. Amherst, NY: Prometheus Books.

Hu, H. C. (1944). The Chinese concepts of "face". *American Anthropologist*, 45–64.

Ivanhoe, P. J. (2020, March 9). Author Interview (R. Shanklin & M. Santoro, Interviewers).

Ivanhoe, P. J., & Van Norden, B. W. (2005). *Readings in classical Chinese philosophy* (2nd ed.). Indianapolis: Hackett.

Kelly, S. (2008, February 11). UPDATE 2-Baxter suspends multi-dose heparin vial production. *Reuters*.

Lee (Li), B. (1971, September 12). *The Pierre Burton show* (P. Burton, Interviewer).

Mèngzi. (2008). *Mengzi* (B. W. Norden, Trans.). Indianapolis: Hackett.

Mozur, P., Scott, M., & Isaac, M. (2017, September). Facebook faces a new world as officials rein in a wild web. *The New York Times*.

Pye, L. W. (1988). *Asian power and politics: The cultural dimensions of authority*. Cambridge, MA: Harvard University Press.

Pye, L. W. (1992). *Chinese negotiating style: Commercial approaches and cultural principles*. Westport, CT: Quorum Books.

Rockoff, J. (2008, March 13). Maryland navtie's expertise led to drug recall. *Baltimore Sun*.

Santoro, M. (2009). *China 2020*. Ithaca, NY: Cornell University Press.

Verstappen, S. (2015). *Chinese business etiquette*. Berkeley: Stone Bridge Press.

Wang, L. (Director). (2019). *The farewell* [Motion Picture]. Retrieved from https://slate.com/culture/2019/07/the-farewell-review-awkwafina-movie.html

Wenzhong, H., Grove, C., & Euping, Z. (2010). *Encountering the Chinese: A modern country, an ancient culture* (3rd ed.). Boston: Intercultural Press.

Xi, J. (2015). *Xi Jinping: The governance of China* (Vol. 1). Shanghai: Shanghai Press.

Xúnzi. (1994). *Xúnzi* (Vol. 3, J. Knoblock, Trans.). Stanford: Stanford University Press.

4

CULTIVATING ETHICAL AGILITY AND EMPLOYING *GUĀNXI* TO PROTECT HUMAN RIGHTS

Just as the idea of face is well-known to foreigners who travel to China, so too is the related concept of *guānxi* (關係), and just as face is often misunderstood and misapplied even by experienced businesspeople, so too is *guānxi*. We begin this chapter by examining the close relationship between the two. We then explore its grounding in traditional Chinese culture and social practice. It is a concept that can seem familiar and easily accessible to Westerners. In reality, however, it requires a deep understanding of nuance and of traditional culture to be properly invoked. When it is poorly understood it can create as much peril as opportunity. Often cynically applied, *guānxi* is frequently misinterpreted as cronyism or, in the worst case, as an excuse to curry favor through bribery. But there is no escaping its crucial role in getting things done, preventing problems from occurring, and fixing problems when they do occur. Thus, cultivating agility in *guānxi* by being able to not only understand it but also to put it into practice is an indispensable skill for Westerners to acquire.

A central theme of this book has been that fluency or Agility in traditional Chinese culture and ethics does not mean "going native" and abandoning your core ethics and business objectives. In previous chapters, we have illustrated this point by showing how knowledge of and Ethical Agility within traditional Chinese ethics in the form of our Ethical Triad can be used to great effect in protecting intellectual property and assuring safety and quality in the manufacturing supply chain, two of the most important ethical and business challenges of operating in China. This chapter puts the utility of cultural fluency to the ultimate test on perhaps the most contentious issue dividing China and the West: human rights. We demonstrate that Ethical Agility in understanding and practicing guānxi can in certain instances constitute the most effective way for companies to fulfill their human rights responsibilities. We consider two well-publicized examples to make our point. In the case of Apple, we show how the agile use of guānxi enabled the company to fix horrific human rights conditions at its principal supplier, Foxconn. By contrast, we consider the hapless response of the National Basketball Association to a Twitter comment by a lone executive about human rights in Hong Kong, which, because inexplicably the NBA had seemingly no guānxi to draw upon, turned into an embarrassing multi-billion-dollar international debacle.

4.1 From face to *guānxi*: creating and sustaining cultural fluency and insider status

It is common to define guānxi as power or influence though social networks. It has also been defined as "networks of favor exchange ties" (Bian, 2019, Yen & Wang, 2011), i.e., networks of personal ties that are close enough to entail norms governing the exchange of favors. The aim of understanding guānxi and putting it to work is for a Western business executive ideally to become sufficiently an "insider" that they can have fruitful relationships with their Chinese counterparts and thereby become part of their networks.

A core way one develops guānxi and thereby cultivates networks of influence is by increasing the face of those with whom one has relationships, and those with whom one wants to have relationships. As those relationships deepen, guānxi develops. One becomes able to rely on others—and be relied upon by others—in many ways, from making a deal beneficial for both sides, to helping fulfill one's duties and obligations to other individuals and firms, and to accessing resources. Because of Interconnectedness, it is not straightforward to clearly distinguish when face is at play versus guānxi. Often, it is both.

Guānxi illustrates each element of our Ethical Triad. First, the inextricability of guānxi and face exemplify Interconnectedness—promoting the face of Chinese counterparts is how one gets in the door and part of how one maintains relationships so that one can participate in guānxi. Second, to accurately understand how guānxi takes different forms in different situations, and to exercise it, requires Awareness of the relevant aspects of face, relationships, and networks. Finally, it exemplifies Context-First insofar as one must first accurately assess the context of each situation one faces before invoking guānxi, including the relationships in play.

An important aspect of guānxi is its variability in relation to hierarchies (a topic we will take up in greater detail in Chapter 5). What counts as right or wrong depends in part upon the hierarchies at work among the relevant parties. As a concrete if simplistic example, consider a mid-level manager. They might be fairly blunt, perhaps even blustery, with their supervisees, because that is seen as an appropriate show of leadership and authority. Yet, the same manager might become very quiet and deferential in the presence of their supervisor, because this is an appropriate show of respect and deference. Because the relationships are different—who is the superior, who is the subordinate—what counts as "correct" behavior varies. To many Westerners, a person who behaves in this manner would be considered two-faced or hypocritical. Westerners often think less of people who treat subordinates poorly while treating bosses unctuously. It is seen as a sign of moral inconsistency. But in Chinese contexts, this is often ethically appropriate, and indeed sometimes even required. This is Context-First in action again, because the question is not "what is the rule for treating others well" as much as "what is the context—in this instance, what hierarchical relationships and which role do I have, such that certain behaviors are appropriate or required." It also requires Ethical Agility insofar as the manager must be able to adjust their outward behavior depending on the situation, in this case the differing roles within hierarchical relationships. Putting all that into practice depends, of course, on the manager having sufficient Awareness regarding these relationships and the associated Chinese cultural norms for determining what is ethically permissible, appropriate, and required.

In addition to hierarchy, the closeness of a relationship is ethically relevant. We have several times in this book noted that one owes more consideration and concern towards one's close friends, family, and longstanding business relations than to new acquaintances, strangers, authorities, and outsiders. A quintessential example of this principle we cited earlier was the contrast between Chinese people being reserved and deferential in many business situations, yet very pushy and disrespectful of personal space when, for example, queuing for a train among relative strangers. We studied the famous so-called "goat problem" (sometimes also called the "sheep problem") in *Analects* 13:18. The question concerns whether a child should disclose to the authorities whether a parent has stolen a goat when it is presumed that the family needed food. The non-Confucian Lord of the state of *She* thinks that uprightness (*zhí*) requires the child to disclose against the parent. According to the standard Chinese perspective, however, the child owes a greater responsibility to a parent with a starving family than to a random authority figure, and uprightness therefore requires the child not to disclose. This story illustrates not only Awareness and the primary importance of Context (in this case, relationships over rules like "don't lie"), but can also help explain certain behaviors that some Western companies find frustrating. To Chinese ways of thinking, the greater responsibility or duty is owed the person with whom one has a relationship (like a longtime business partner or someone within the company), rather than a stranger, foreigner, or random authority figure.

The importance of closeness in a personal relationship—or lack thereof— also helps explain why many American and European businesspeople report trouble getting Chinese partners to honor agreements, especially contracts (Saxon, 2006). The foreigner is like the authorities in the goat story; the Western business partner is neither family, nor trusted friend, nor insider (Feldman, 2013). We start out as unknown outsiders, and foreigners on top of that. To further complicate matters, the confidence and even bluster so often prized in Western business contexts is interpreted as insulting. The Western businessperson expressing what they think of as overt confidence is, in fact, addressing the Chinese partner in the way the Chinese partner thinks it is appropriate to treat an underling (De Menthe, 2013). The Ethically Agile Westerner accurately understands the situation and applies the appropriate principles or values.

The tension a Westerner might feel about favoring family and friends in various contexts is considerably lessened if not absent altogether in China. As business ethicist Tom Donaldson has written, whether nepotism in foreign subsidiaries is tolerable or violative of a company's core values is one of the most common and vexing issues of international business (Donaldson, 1996). Whereas a Westerner might hold fairness or equal treatment as fundamental ethical values, and be taught to avoid nepotism, to Chinese perspectives the closeness and length of the relationship are primary ethical considerations. This is a central cultural notion that drives the Chinese concept of *guānxi*. Status within your relationships and the networks they form determine ethical standing as insider or outsider, close relation or distant (Buderi & Huang, 2006). That, in turn, affects how much consideration you deserve, both in terms of ethics and etiquette (because of Interconnectedness). Are you to be dismissed like Xi Jinping dismissed Mark Zuckerberg when Zuckerberg asked Xi to name his child, or do you deserve something more, like being kindly and apologetically let down, or offered an acceptable alternative?

As we have noted, Westerners (and many Chinese businesspeople as well) misunderstand and misapply *guānxi*, sometimes deliberately and with corrupt intentions. One form of such "bad *guānxi*" concerns the intentional use of social networks to generate illicit favors or participate in corruption or excessive nepotism (Nolan, 2011). Out of respect for others and the ties one has with them, one is expected to do certain favors for others within one's *guānxi* network. However, this can go too far, as when agreements are made with clearly unqualified individuals or firms that flout quality or safety standards. A dramatic example of this occurred in Shanghai in 2009 when a nearly-completed 13-story building fell over on its side (Woetzel & Towson, 2017). Its foundations were reportedly unable to sustain the stresses that occurred as construction continued in the construction complex in which the building was located, including on an adjacent parking garage.

A second form of "bad *guānxi*" occurs when *guānxi* is invoked as a means to justify practices that not only violate Western legal-ethical norms, but Chinese cultural-ethical norms as well (Feng, 2005, Barboza, 2006, The Economist, 2007). For example, Chinese bankers sometimes creatively reinterpret the norms of *guānxi*, whether with clear knowledge of what they are doing or not, to justify illicit behaviors and activities including money laundering and embezzlement (Nolan, 2011, p. 3367). If you bring up the subject with any businessperson, foreign or domestic, big company or small, the reaction will almost uniformly be one of resignation over the overwhelming pervasiveness of bribes and kickbacks both in private business transactions and in dealings with the government. The sobering truth is that foreign firms seem to be as much perpetrators as victims of corruption and, to justify their behavior, they will often mischaracterize their corruption as simply following what they allege to be the norms of *guānxi* (BBC, 2005).

But their use of the term *guānxi* to justify their participation in an informal system of bribery and corruption is not an authentic norm and has little basis in Chinese ethics.

Guānxi must go beyond simple favor exchanges to be authentic. In Chinese culture contexts, business deals are to be built on personal non-superficial relationships, the kinds on which trust as well as reputations can be built (Yen, Barnes, and Wang, 2011, Bian, 2019, pp. 28–65). That is how deals are made that benefit the parties involved, while simultaneously the most ethical practices and the best responses in the face of disaster are achieved (Rosen, 1999, Pearce & Robinson, 2000). Guānxi takes time to develop and best develops organically, ideally over the course of years (Barnes, Yen, & Zhou, 2011). As we discussed in connection with face earlier, a common concern in response to such advice is that it would take too much time. In essence, however, that is already a declaration of failure from the Westerner, not only because of the persistent importance of *guānxi*, but also because Chinese perspectives on time are very different from broadly Western, and especially American, perspectives. If you're thinking to yourself "this is complicated, this is weird, it would take too long," then you have "drawn the line" like Confucius' student Ran Qiu, who had decided that the Confucian Way of living was too difficult before giving it a solid try (Ivanhoe & Van Norden, 2005). It bears repeating that investing in relationships is the price of doing business in China: "if you do not have time to learn about China, then you do not have time to succeed in China" (Hupert, 2014). Though some things in China infamously happen at incredible speed, such as construction in cities, one should assume that Chinese partners are always playing the long game. To insist that building personal relationships—as part of business—takes too much time is to prevent oneself from being able to understand and engage Chinese mindsets, effectively sabotaging one's own opportunities.

One concern worth mentioning about the feasibility of Western individuals and businesses engaging in effective relationship-building and the exercise of *guānxi* is that favor-exchange and gift-giving are often restricted or forbidden by home-country legal strictures such as the US Foreign Corrupt Practices Act (FCPA). This, however, can be overcome. There are many stories where scripts as simple as the following were sufficient to cultivate and preserve relationships: "my government does not allow me to give you the gift or recognition you deserve, for that I am sorry and mean no disrespect." Experienced business executives report that acknowledging Chinese norms and participating in even modest gift-giving goes a long way toward maintaining relationships and guānxi, even when the value of the gift is lower than would be the norm within China (Hupert, 2014, Verstappen, 2015).

Establishing corporate-level guānxi with international reach is not easy, but it can be accomplished. Israeli tech firms have, for example, successfully incorporated guānxi into their relations with Chinese counterparts (Berger, Herstein, Silbiger, & Barnes, 2015). Two crucial takeaways of Israeli experiences are discussed by Yanjie Bian. First, Israeli managers describe the relationships with Chinese businesspeople in personal terms: "talk openly as friends," "have a brotherly feeling towards the contact person," and "would try my best to help out my contact person when he/she is in need" (Bian, 2019, p. 165). Second, even though gift-giving as practiced in Chinese business contexts appears to many Israeli businesspeople as bribery—as it does to many Europeans and Americans—they "understand the importance of giving a gift as a ritual of empathy or fellow feeling . . . how to give a gift is more important than what the actual gift is" (Bian, 2019, p. 165). Thus, Israeli businesspeople find success while avoiding bribery concerns by focusing less on the monetary value of the gift—as one would have, traditionally—and focusing instead on cultivating their conduct in giving smaller gifts in ways that are face-saving, and hence relationship-building, in regard to their Chinese counterparts.

Of course, in the fast-paced world of business it is not always possible to invest years in the hopes of securing a deal or a contract. For long-term supply and joint-venture relationships, it is essential to invest significant time, but for more episodic business relationships it is still important to slow down with Chinese counterparts and put in some time. The investment of time won't always pan out, but it is essential if one is to have any hope of securing important deals. Private equity investor Brewer Stone has been traveling to China for three decades. He explains how much effort is required to attempt to establish guānxi in a compressed time frame and also the limits of what it can do—in essence, it can help make the deal possible but it is not enough in itself to seal the deal. "Will mastering the nuances of Chinese traditions and business culture guarantee success? I would say absolutely, but only to a point." He offers the following story to illustrate the limits of guānxi:

I made a great deal of effort to be culturally sensitive in building a relationship with the Chairman of one of China's largest and most innovative electrical metering companies—and at a personal level it was a very rewarding relationship. We had tea ceremonies together, took slow walks around the shores of the scenic, willow tree ringed West Lake in Hangzhou, had numerous long and complex meals, and toasts, discussions of Chinese history, food, language, etc. On the business side too, he seemed to really value my and my firm's advice. But did we really become deep friends, like the people he grew up with or went through the Cultural Revolution with? No way. And in the end, he made business decisions in a very practical way that took significant account of a broad swath of interests—his own and local government looming large—and did not make deal closing easy.

(Stone, Interview, 2020)

4.2 Business responsibility for human rights in China

In this chapter, we discuss how fluency in traditional culture, in particular guānxi, can help foreign companies to fulfill their human rights responsibilities. Before doing so, however, it is worth reflecting on the broad array of human rights challenges in China and the moral basis for the expectation that companies should do something about them.

There are, generally speaking, two kinds of human rights responsibilities companies have in China. The first set, which is easier to pinpoint but nonetheless difficult to satisfy, emanates from China's role as the world's factory floor and includes worker conditions, labor rights, and the environmental impacts of manufacturing. A second, more diverse and complex set of issues arise from the heavy-handed rule of the Chinese Communist Party. Rights such as free speech, assembly, internet freedom, privacy violations, and citizen surveillance are but the most obvious examples of the human rights issues arising from China's authoritarian political regime. These two sorts of issues can overlap, as, for example, in the case of the union-organizing rights of workers or the repression of Uighurs in the Xinjiang region.

Why should business have any responsibility for human rights? After all, executives of private companies manage assets owned by shareholders and thus, in many Western jurisdictions, legally owe fiduciary duties to competently manage those assets and return profits for shareholders. The extreme version of this duty was infamously enunciated by Milton Friedman who claimed that the "sole responsibility of business is to increase its profits"

(Friedman, 1970). In recent years, however, the idea that corporations have moral responsibilities other than maximizing profits has become an increasingly accepted notion. A watershed moment in this process was the unanimous adoption by the United Nations Human Rights Council in 2011 of the *Guiding Principles on Business and Human Rights* (widely known informally as the "UNGPs"). They provide, among other things, that businesses have the responsibility to "respect" human rights: "this means that they should avoid infringing on the human rights of others and should address adverse human rights impacts with which they are involved" (United Nations, 2011a, Principle 11). This responsibility requires that businesses "seek to prevent or mitigate adverse human rights impacts that are directly linked to their operations . . . even if they have not contributed to those impacts" (United Nations, 2011b, Principle 13b). The UNGPs might be said to possess a certain moral authority by virtue of their reflecting, in some measure, an imperfect consensus of the "global community" about the human rights responsibilities of business. However, it is worth reflecting upon the philosophical foundations that underpin the moral responsibility to respect human rights, which is a particular instance of the moral duty of business to act in a socially responsible manner.

The moral argument for corporate social responsibility can be constructed from a number of philosophical premises. One widely influential approach is based on the idea of a "social contract."[12] Broadly speaking, the idea of a corporate social contract is based on the political social contract in the writings of John Locke, Jean-Jacques Rousseau, and Thomas Hobbes (D'Agostino, 2019). The "social contract" as applied to business is meant to describe the relationship of trust existing between corporations and society (Donaldson & Dunfee, 1999). The very existence of a corporation as a legal "person" is made possible by society. Society also enacts and enforces the legal norms and institutions that protect private property, the accumulation of capital, and profits. In return for what society makes possible for them, corporations are accountable to society. They have a reciprocal "contractual" moral duty to operate in a manner that benefits society, i.e., in a socially responsible manner. Global businesses are incorporated and enjoy legal

---

12   In the business ethics literature, the seminal work applying social contract theory to the human rights responsibilities of multinational corporations is Donaldson (1989). For other influential approaches, see Wettstein (2009) and Hsieh (2015).

personhood within the jurisdictions and territories of their "home" states. They also operate abroad in multiple jurisdictions or "host" countries, such as China, where they might manufacture or sell their products. Multinational businesses thus enjoy various rights and privileges in both home and host countries. In return, they owe duties to act in a socially responsible manner in both the home and host countries in which they enjoy legal existence and operate (Donaldson, 1989).

A corporation's moral responsibility for human rights is a particular instance of its duty to act in a socially responsible manner. Human rights are

> rights of such importance that they impose correlative duties on actors beyond a nation's borders. To call something a "human right" is to say that it imposes duties upon others across national borders to honor that right. Human rights are moral rights. Human rights exist regardless of whether a particular national government in actuality protects those rights.
>
> (Santoro, 2009)

Of course, the existence of human rights that impose moral duties with international reach begs a number of crucial questions. Who owes what human rights duties? What duties does business owe with respect to human rights, as opposed to duties owed by other entities such as governments and non-governmental organizations? Just as the existence of corporate human rights duties required philosophical justification for moral persuasiveness, so too does the assignment of particular duties to any particular actors, including businesses (Santoro, 2000).

One way to draw the extent and limits of corporate responsibility for human rights is the idea that business should shoulder its "Fair Share" of the burden of protecting human rights violations and remedying such violations when they occur (Santoro, 2015). The "Fair Share" theory acknowledges that the human rights duties of companies operating in China and elsewhere can be costly in financial terms and strategic consequences, and, therefore, should not be expected to amount to the equivalent of a blank check.[13]

---

13 The argument is sometimes made that corporate social responsibility is a win-win situation by which it is implied that "doing good" or behaving in a socially responsible way will result in "doing well" or making profits. This question of whether ethics "pays" has been discussed,

To be sustainable, corporate social responsibility must be compatible with a healthy income statement and balance sheet. This is not to say that some business activities that violate human rights should not be undertaken regardless of their impact on profits. Indeed, in the case of China, some have argued that it is immoral for multinational corporations to do business there under any circumstances. Although it eventually returned, in the 1990s Levi-Strauss, for example, initially planned to withdraw from China on the grounds that human rights violations were so serious and pervasive that it would violate their code of conduct to manufacture jeans there (Schoenberger, 1998).

Although a discussion of the full scope of what a Fair Share theory of human rights would require in every instance is beyond the scope of this discussion, in the case of China two bedrock principles apply. First, consistent with the UNGPs, companies are responsible for protecting the human rights of workers throughout their supply chain. We will explore this issue in our discussion of the Apple Foxconn case in the following sections. Second, when they can do so effectively, companies and their agents have a duty to speak up (but not, as we will argue, necessarily "out") about general human rights conditions, a subject we take up in our discussion of the National Basketball Association.

The idea that Ethical Agility in the form of *guānxi* should be employed in furtherance of fulfilling human rights duties is consistent with the idea of companies doing their "fair share." When businesses practice Ethical Agility in protecting human rights they accomplish two things: they increase their effectiveness and, at the same time, they can reduce the potential financial impacts of retaliation from the government. We well understand why this might not sit well with some human rights advocates who seek to pressure business to act in a responsible manner. Speaking out and publicly standing up for human rights often does not entail much in the way of cultural subtlety or compromise. Among the most enduring images of human rights activism are a solitary man standing in front of a tank in Tiananmen Square, Nelson Mandela in a Robben Island jail, or Colin Kaepernick kneeling during the US national anthem. The idea of quiet diplomacy through culturally

---

debated, and empirically studied for decades with no clear-cut answer emerging. For a thoughtful and sophisticated take on how to think about the question of whether ethics "pays," see Paine (2002), Chapter 2.

sensitive communication would not seem to fit within this paradigm of human rights advocacy and progress. However, for businesses operating in and with China, the protection of human rights more often than not is more effectively accomplished in the detailed conversations about management and operating procedures that happen outside the glare of publicity. It is in such conversations that our Ethical Triad and Ethical Agility in the use of guānxi in particular become useful in promoting and protecting human rights.

A final word to be said about cultural fluency and human rights is that inevitably something is going to get lost in translation because of the uncertain and evolving status of rights generally, and human rights in particular. Some have argued that from traditional Chinese perspectives, rights are not a salient concept upon which individuals and organizations interact with one another (Ihara, 2004, pp. 11–30). Ann Kent, in her seminal work describing China's perspectives on human rights, observed that higher priorities in China have been and seem to continue to be: social order; economic mobility and economic growth; a sense of being respected as a national power on the world stage; harmony within one's social groups and hierarchies, and; staying out of trouble with the government (Kent, 1993).[14] Though things may change in time—a recent dissertation argues that the right understanding of human dignity, which is held in common between Eastern and Western religious-philosophical contexts, can ground more productive rights-conversations in East Asia and especially China (Ang, 2019)—this rights-disconnect is here to stay, at least for the foreseeable future.

To appreciate how cultural fluency can still help achieve more positive human rights outcomes even in a country where rights are still generally seen as a foreign notion, the work of John Kamm and the San Francisco-based Dui Hua Foundation is exemplary. John Kamm is a businessman who has been traveling to China for five decades. In 2004, he was awarded a MacArthur Foundation "genius" award for his human rights work. Dui Hua has successfully intervened on behalf of hundreds of prisoners of conscience in China. Kamm regularly travels to China and meets with high-ranking government

---

14 For those interested in a deeper dive on the question of the compatibility of East Asian philosophy and human rights, excellent places to start are Bauer and Bell (1999) and Angle (2002).

leaders, often raising extremely sensitive subjects with them. Kamm says "in discussing sensitive issues like political prisoners with Chinese officials, I have found that it is best to keep the meetings as low-key and informal as possible" (Kamm, Interview, 2020). Kamm also emphasizes that one of his major goals is to help China be better understood and respected in the West. "Most important," says Kamm,

> I try to convince my counterparts that releasing someone that the government sees as an enemy holds benefits for China, being as specific as possible. I approach the enterprise with respect and in a spirit of friendship and trust. I am results-oriented. I never criticize senior officials by name, and when the Chinese government does good, I find ways to recognize it.

Kamm's approach of mixing *guān*xi with respectful criticism works. When a Chinese official was asked about Kamm, they replied, "He loves China. He shows respect. He is constructive and realistic" (Santoro, 2009).

4.3 Apple and the Foxconn suicides: employing *guānxi* to protect human rights in the supply chain

To illustrate the usefulness of *guānxi* for addressing human rights issues in the supply chain, we diagnose what was done right and what could have been done better by Apple during and following a disturbing string of suicides at its main Chinese supplier, the Taiwanese-owned Foxconn. Beginning in January 2010, and continuing with frightening regularity throughout the year, there was a series of at least 14 suicides, all of younger workers, at the so-called "Foxconn City" industrial park in Shenzhen, where the bulk of Apple's iPhones are manufactured, as well as products for Hewlett-Packard, Motorola, Nokia, IBM, and Cisco (Rothlin & McCann, 2015, pp. 158–161).[15]

---

15 Pressures that led to the suicides in 2010–2011 have recently been ratcheted up in the era of COVID-19 when workers are expected to increase productivity and maintain social distancing. In March 2020, China Labor Watch (CLW) reported that a Foxconn worker, rumored to have contracted COVID-19, committed suicide by jumping from the 11th floor of a Foxconn dormitory (Bennet, 2020).

At first, Foxconn took a no-comment approach to these suicides by not admitting that there was a problem, and (at least publicly) treating the initial four suicides as isolated incidents. This was a face-saving move insofar as it avoided admitting failure while suggesting causes that did not point back to Foxconn. However, after the fourth suicide, Foxconn acted. One step was to admit to poor management of new staff. Like most workers in large coastal cities in China, the overwhelming majority of Foxconn workers are from poor rural backgrounds, and are, in many cases, earning money to support not just themselves but family who may be quite distant (Rothlin & McCann, 2015, p. 160). As a result, this population presents distinctive ethical and management challenges, including pressure to work long hours combined with a profound fear of failure. This, together with spectacular global demand from clients such as Apple, led to workers working far beyond local overtime regulations, often without overtime pay (Rothlin & McCann, 2015, pp. 162–163). This scandal, coming as it did just a few years after an ongoing controversy about alleged sweatshop conditions at Foxconn, led to significant notoriety, as well as attention from the Chinese government. Presumably in part to save face in light of international scrutiny and criticism, the Chinese government turned its eye on Foxconn and began an official inquiry of working conditions there (Wang & Zhan, 2010).

Apple has an unusually close commercial relationship with Foxconn. iPhones account for over 50 percent of Foxconn's revenue, and around 60 percent of Apple's sales (Kanematsu, 2017). Reports suggest that several of Foxconn's global clients, Apple among them, approached Foxconn to work collaboratively to address the problems that were leading to the suicides (Kanematsu, 2017, The Economist, 2010). It is in precisely such situations that an accurate and nuanced understanding of *guānxi*, together with the skill to apply it—Ethical Agility—is needed, to manage risk and save lives. Evidence that Apple, especially under Tim Cook, possesses significant Ethical Agility comes from several of Apple's outward behaviors toward Foxconn, both in challenging times and more ordinary times. One behavior is the personal touch of sending Mr. Cook to China several times over a period of many years, first as COO and then as CEO, to meet with executives and workers alike, as well as government officials (BBC, 2012, Vincent, 2016). To Chinese perspectives, sending a very high-ranking person indicates how seriously Apple takes the relationship between the firms. In challenging times, such as following the 2010–2011 suicides, it also indicates to Chinese counterparts and government officials how seriously Apple regards the problem to be. This serves to put the spotlight on any Foxconn response, which means they will be more likely to be more compliant, not only to preserve face on the global stage, but to be seen in a posture of problem-solving and cooperation with the world's most valuable brand. All of these practices serve to promote face for Foxconn workers, executives, and even its CEO, Terry Gou. This is because they present Gou as a key collaborator working with one of the world's most powerful companies and famous CEOs to help solve problems, rather than as a (mere) contracted manufacturer and "gadget assembler" (Gurman, 2019).

Here is yet another place where face and *guānxi* interact: the promotion of face serves as a cornerstone and powerful motivator for maintaining the relationship with Apple and its cooperative tenor. The Apple-Foxconn experience thus offers validation for our proposition that cultivating and maintaining *guānxi* is a highly useful resource to get Chinese counterparts and partner firms to improve transparency, raise their accountability, and act quickly when human rights problems and other problems arise that need to be addressed. The point is not to dismiss the importance of vigilant (and, better yet, independent external) monitoring of labor conditions that has become the gold standard for assuring human rights compliance. What we are saying is that if a company wants to prevent human rights problems from emerging in the supply chain in the first place, and deal effectively with problems when they arise, then it is critical that it fully embrace the importance cultivating *guānxi* and, more generally, appreciate of the underlying dynamics of traditional Chinese culture (Santoro, 2003).

To be sure, human rights concerns and allegations continue to plague Foxconn and Apple, but the blueprint for prevention and cure has been established. In 2019, China Labor Watch (CLW) alleged that despite previous investigations and promises to rectify the situation, Foxconn had temporary staff known as dispatch workers comprising around half of the workforce, whereas Chinese labor law stipulates a maximum of 10 percent (Gurman, 2019). Temporary staff are often hired in large numbers to meet seasonal demand. They receive fewer protections than regular workers. In addition, CLW alleged, resignations were not approved during peak production periods, some temporary staff did not receive promised bonuses, student workers were doing overtime during peak season despite regulations that prohibit this, and some workers were putting in over 100 overtime hours each month, where Chinese labor law limits that to 36 hours (Choudhury, 2019). Adding to the complexity of the situation is the fact that many workers want to work overtime to make more money. Thus, there is significant demand from workers for Foxconn to break Chinese labor laws and to tread into territory that violates human rights (Gurman, 2019).

To address these new allegations, Apple continues to rely on longstanding *guānxi* in the way it interacts with Foxconn, maintaining an attitude and posture of respect and collaboration while avoiding any finger-pointing or blame. As an example, consider Apple's official public response to the allegations:

> Apple said that, after conducting an investigation, it found the "percentage of [temporary] workers exceeded our standards" and that it is "working closely with Foxconn to resolve this issue." It added that when it finds issues, it works with suppliers to "take immediate corrective action." Foxconn Technology Group also confirmed the dispatch worker violation following an operational review.
>
> (Gurman, 2019)

This approach has been consistent in Apple's public commentary regarding its relationship with Foxconn and Gou, from 2010 to the present day. The effectiveness of this approach is reflected in Foxconn's rhetoric following the CLW allegations. Instead of evasion and denial, the company said its

> work to address the issues identified in our Zhengzhou facility continues and we will closely monitor the situation. We will not hesitate to take any additional steps that might be required to meet the high standards we set for our operations.
>
> (Gurman, 2019)

In sum, addressing the 2010 crises at Foxconn in the way Apple did, it helped to develop their most important global supplier into a company that effectively responds and communicates with Western audiences on human rights challenges. This is no small achievement in protecting human rights.

It should be noted that, while Apple has been successful in addressing human rights concerns in its manufacturing supply chain at Foxconn—reflecting that, unlike Google and Facebook, it is primarily a hardware company—it has been less adept at addressing more human rights issues emanating from the software side of its business. For example, the company has come under criticism from activist shareholders and human rights advocates for removing virtual networking (VPN) apps—which enable users to avoid China's internet censorship and access foreign news outlets—from its App store. Responding to this criticism in September 2020, Apple published a human rights policy, "Our Commitment to Human Rights," in which it claimed, without much explanation or apparent justification, to be "based on" the UNGPs (Apple, Inc. 2020). While the policy, which fails to mention China, acknowledged "the critical importance of an open society in which information flows freely," this affirmation was undercut by the company's dubious claim in the next breath that "we're convinced the best way we can continue to promote openness is to remain engaged, even where we may disagree with a country's laws." Apple's "UNGP-washing" human rights policy was, to say the least, a disappointing pronouncement for a company that, under CEO Tim Cook's leadership, has claimed to be a defender of the freedom of speech and privacy of its customers. Because of its decades of experience and plethora of strong relationships with Chinese government officials, Apple is certainly capable of taking a stronger stand on internet freedom and it most certainly has a moral duty to do so.

the system of social networks & influential relationships in business & other dealings

4.4 The NBA *guānxi* deficit: on defense rather than defending human rights

If Apple's handling of the Foxconn suicides stands as an example of how *guānxi* can be used to protect human rights, the National Basketball Association's (NBA) handling of a pro-Hong Kong democracy tweet by a team official illustrates how badly things can go for companies that fail to cultivate *guānxi*. The NBA first went to China in 1985. At first, it practically gave away broadcast rights, but Chinese interest in the sport was strong and eventually in 2015 Tencent signed a five-year, $700 million deal to stream NBA games and related content (Ozanian, 2018, Beam, 2020). From 2004 to 2019, estimated revenues from Chinese viewership and sponsorship rose from $9.5 million to $500 million per year. Around 2008, the NBA set up a subsidiary, NBA China, that a decade later was reportedly worth over $4 billion (Ozanian, 2018). Mark Fischer, former managing director of NBA China, said that part of the reason for establishing a subsidiary there was not just to help manage a complex business, but "to increase the NBA's influence and connections in the corridors of Chinese government power" (Beam, 2020).

The attempt to build a relationship on which it could draw failed, however. Acute need for such a relationship came on Friday, 4 October 2019, when Daryl Morey, the general manager of the Houston Rockets, tweeted, "Fight for Freedom, Stand with Hong Kong." He soon deleted it, but the damage had already been done. Within approximately 48 hours, Chinese companies, such as the Li Ning shoe company and the Shanghai Pudong Development Bank, pulled out of sponsorship deals with the Rockets, the Chinese Basketball Association (CBA) stated that it had stopped "communication and cooperation" with the team, and Tencent dropped broadcasts of Rockets games (Beam, 2020). The CBA suspended ties with the team even though the president of the CBA is the former Rockets superstar Yao Ming (The New York Times Editorial Board, 2019).

While reactions from China were swift and strong, responses from the NBA were in utter disarray. Rockets owner Tilman Fertitta told ESPN "we're here to play basketball and not to offend anybody," but league Commissioner Adam Silver vaguely defended Daryl Morey's right to free speech (The New York Times Editorial Board, 2019). Players James Harden and LeBron James—whose financial interests depend significantly on business with China—apologized for the tweet, indicating great appreciation for their Chinese fans. This, however, resulted in their jerseys being burned by Hong Kong protestors (The New York Times Editorial Board, 2019, Beam, 2020).

Senators and members of the US Congress, conservative and liberal alike, denounced the NBA for caving in to China and its hypocrisy on human rights. The NBA, its leaders, coaches, and stars have been vocal for many years about racial justice, increasingly so following the mounting deaths of unarmed black men and women at the hands of American police, as well as the election of President Trump in 2016 (Beam, 2020). And yet, in the case of China, the NBA found itself in the posture of muting an executive expressing support for human rights quite plainly because of the financial consequences. In early 2020, NBA games were suspended because of COVID-19, and after nearly six months it appeared that the controversy had died down. However, in May 2020, when the league was set to play basketball again, China Central TV (CCTV) issued a statement indicating that it would not resume airing NBA games, saying: "On questions of China's sovereignty, CCTV's attitude is strict, clear, and consistent" (Beam, 2020).

The fallout over Daryl Morey's tweet raises many difficult ethical questions. As a US citizen, Morey has the right to express his opinion, and from a human rights perspective, the people of Hong Kong have a right to free expression and self-determination. However, from the Chinese perspective, he was touching a raw nerve. When the Qing Dynasty lost the Opium Wars in the 19th century, it was forced to cede Hong Kong to the British as a trading post until 1997, when it reverted back to China in an agreement with the British that was intended to preserve legal and political freedoms for the next 50 years. Joe Tsai (Chinese national, co-founder of Alibaba, and controlling owner of the Brooklyn Nets team) expressed his view of the offensive nature of Morey's tweet in an open letter (Tsai, 2019).

The NBA found itself navigating through the Charybdis of human rights and the Scylla of Chinese nationalism. This is not an enviable position but it is an inevitable one for any major global brand operating in China. Most such companies deliberately manage to steer away from any public comments about political freedoms (or lack thereof) in China. The Morey tweet, however, thrust the NBA right into the middle of a complex issue of global ethics. What placed them on the horns of the dilemma was their commitment to racial justice and human rights. The NBA could not sidestep the issue the way the English Soccer League (cravenly but effectively) did when, on Instagram, Arsenal midfielder Mesut Özil criticized human rights transgressions against Uighur in western China (Ames, 2019). His team followed a standard China crisis playbook of issuing a face-saving apology, then waiting for the controversy to blow over (Dreyer, 2019). Arsenal immediately distanced itself, claiming that the post expressed a personal opinion and reiterated the team's policy of not "involving itself in politics" (Ames, 2019). China and many Chinese fans took this as a satisfactorily face- and relationship-saving apology (Beam, 2020). Perhaps, if instead of a team official it had been a player who spoke out on human rights, the NBA might have had available to it a version of the Arsenal playbook, though it would strain credulity to claim it had a policy of not "involving itself in politics."

When it came time to act with purpose, the NBA was woefully unprepared. They allowed a single tweet to turn into an international debacle for the NBA. They were unable to maintain their commitment to human rights while preserving their financial interests. What they lacked at the critical moment, and in the years leading up to it, was an understanding of the principles of our Ethical Triad, and, in particular, the indispensability of acquiring Awareness and Ethical Agility in face and *guānxi*.

Before we describe a few things that the NBA could have done better, we hasten to add that the Daryl Morey tweet was not the ideal way for the NBA to be staking out a position on human rights in China. In fact, it would be hard to imagine a worse posture for taking on the issue because of its highly public nature. In short, to use a sports metaphor, they were playing defense on human rights and were in no position to defend human rights. Though Daryl Morey is not top-brass NBA leadership, his position as general manager will, to many Chinese and East Asian perspectives, render him a leader and as a result someone who bears special responsibilities as a public representative of his team and league. To put out a publicly critical tweet meant that, to typical Chinese perspectives, Morey had taken it upon himself to step into the ring of international diplomacy. It is unsurprising that the Chinese government and business organizations moved to save face by reacting not just to a lone individual's tweet but to the organizations Morey took it upon himself to represent: the Rockets and, to a lesser extent, even the NBA. Morey's tweet eroded face by expressing disrespect for Chinese leaders, the CBA, NBA China, and Chinese fans: "if you disrespect our country, we can live without your games" (Beam, 2020).

So, what could the NBA have done better? First, before we discuss their lack of Ethical Agility, it was shocking to see that they lacked even basic institutional knowledge about China and human rights conditions there. Even considering that the Morey tweet was a thorny way to have to introduce the issue, it is still remarkable that after 35 years of doing business there, the NBA found itself tongue-tied about their position on human rights. With their vague and contradictory remarks, it seemed like NBA executives had never thought about the issue and were making it up as they went along. The NBA is a global brand, and like every other global brand these days, it needs to have a sophisticated and informed human rights capacity in the C-Suite. Indeed, if the NBA had this capacity, it might have averted the Daryl Morey tweet in the first place. Like the messaging on any other important political issue in a global business organization, the NBA could have controlled how and when it would say something about human rights in China. Put another way, controlling what league executives say publicly about human rights is a lot more palatable if the NBA organization had a clear and responsible corporate voice and policy about human rights. Instead of squandering all its potential influence playing defense, it could possibly have had a positive impact or at least registered its opinion respectfully.

In addition to being substantively unprepared, a second and even more debilitating factor was the absence of sufficiently close relationships between the NBA, its subsidiary NBA China, Chinese broadcasting companies including CCTV, and the Chinese government. After 35 years, and despite setting up a subsidiary with the express purpose of cultivating such relationships 12 years ago, the NBA simply did not have the Ethical Agility with relationships and *guānxi* needed to weather this type of storm. Back in the 1980s and 1990s, as the size of the business opportunity in China became clear, NBA top brass should have made it a larger priority to cultivate relationships with its Chinese broadcasting partners and the Chinese government. This was the playbook followed by Tim Cook at Apple, Bill Gates at Microsoft, and Hank Paulson at Goldman Sachs. The NBA instead treated China as an ATM machine, raking in the profits but not making any sincere efforts to develop meaningful relationships.

Third, while we agree that setting up NBA China was on point, it was ineffectually implemented. That organization needed to be led by Chinese nationals who had their own networks of relationships—and hence *guānxi*—which are required to both get things done and manage disasters. Bringing in Michael Ma in 2020 to try to assuage the Chinese government was the right idea, but far too little too late. This hollowed-out and mismanaged corporate presence in China is a sign that the NBA was running a bare-bones operation in China without making significant investments in building relationships and *guānxi*. After 35 years in China, the NBA remained strangers even though their games and players had loyal followings among what has been estimated to be up to 500 million fans. It was an extraordinarily incompetent disconnect between commercial importance and managerial attention.

Even under the best of circumstances, it requires substantial Ethical Agility to effectively negotiate the terrain of human rights in China. Only with strong and longstanding relationships of trust can a global company operating in China hope to have any chance of saying something substantive, much less making a positive impact by doing its fair share on general human rights conditions. Within such relationships and by drawing on *guānxi*, delicate conversations can be had about Muslim players sympathizing with Uighur and Western players sympathizing with pro-democracy movements in Hong Kong and elsewhere, while acknowledging the awkwardness of foreigners commenting on Chinese politics and society so as to preserve sufficient face that these relationships can continue and weather storms.

If the NBA could not remotely expect to magically turn China into a liberal democracy through quiet diplomacy, it could at least have set the stage to lobby for the freedom of jailed dissidents or persecuted minorities. If this seems like too modest an expectation, consider what the cumulative effect would be if dozens of similarly commercially significant foreign firms followed the same playbook. Moreover, modest expectations about businesses speaking out about general human rights conditions in China that have nothing to do with its operations should be understood in the context of the idea of doing its "fair share." Governments and non-governmental organizations such as Human Rights Watch and Amnesty International are better positioned to speak not just up, but out, and press the case for human rights reforms. Business is not in a position to take the lead on such external international pressure for human rights reform in China, but it does have a responsibility to support such efforts.

4.5 Final thoughts: moving from basic to intermediate cultural fluency

Doing business both successfully and more ethically in China is not just a matter of understanding our three-part framework of Context-First, Interconnectedness, and Awareness, plus the twin phenomena of face and *guānxi*. Success requires putting these into practice by adapting to the various concrete situations in which we find ourselves—what we call Ethical Agility. Roughly, this amounts to having the intellectual and emotional fluidity not only to recognize a different ethical system for what it is, but to navigate that system effectively.

In this chapter, we connected Ethical Agility with face to the all-important process of cultivating and maintaining relationships in Chinese business contexts. Fluency with these relationships allows Western businesspeople to exercise influence through those relationships, and through the networks in which Chinese counterparts participate. This is Ethical Agility with *guānxi*, perhaps the most famous (or notorious) challenge for Westerners doing business in China. We discussed what happens when *guānxi* is misapplied; when it is expertly applied, as in the Apple case; and when it is wholly missing, as in the NBA case.

We are not suggesting that Westerners can develop perfect skill in *guānxi*—after all, many Chinese folks make mistakes in *guānxi*. There is neither a presumption nor an expectation of perfection; one is still a foreigner. Any sincere effort combined with moderate familiarity with Chinese culture, customs, and language go a long way towards opening the door to the more sustained relations that we have explained how to cultivate and maintain. A modicum of Agility with relationships and *guānxi* is necessary to avoid classic pitfalls of doing business in China, such as deals suddenly falling apart or ending up with unfavorable contracts. Moreover, Agility with relationships and *guānxi* is the number-one way to increase transparency and accountability, and, in doing so, further reduce the chances that a problem will boil over into a disaster, while improving cooperation with your firm when crises do occur.

A central theme of this book has been that fluency or Agility in traditional Chinese culture and ethics does not mean "going native" and abandoning your core ethics and business goals. Instead, we have argued, Agility in face and *guānxi* can in certain instances constitute the most effective way to achieve ethical and business objectives. We have put this claim to the test in some of the most challenging ethical issues foreign business encounter in China—protecting intellectual property, assuring safety and quality in the manufacturing supply chain, and human rights. In the next and final chapter, we go beyond the basic concepts of face and *guānxi* and dive more deeply into other important aspects of traditional Chinese ethics. Unlike face and *guānxi*, however, the ideas we discuss in the next chapter are less familiar to most business businesspeople in China. Nonetheless, as we shall see, they are an important part of the Chinese ethical mindset and form a backdrop to contemporary Chinese business.

References

Ames, N. (2019, December 13). Arsenal distance themselves from Mesut Özil comments on Uighurs' plight. *The Guardian*, p. 1.

Ang, F. T. (2019). *Humanizing the business and human rights (BHR) debate: A study based on the Asian philosophies of Buddhism and Confucianism.* St Gallen: University of St. Gallen, School of Management, Economics, Law, Social Sciences and International Affairs.

Angle, S. (2002). *Human rights and Chinese thought: A cross-cultural inquiry.* New York: Cambridge University Press.

Apple, Inc. (2020, August). Apple human rights policy. Retrieved August 6, 2020, from https://s2.q4cdn.com/470004039/files/doc_downloads/gov_docs/Apple-Human-Rights-Policy.pdf

Barboza, D. (2006, December 1). Ripples keep spreading in a Chinese bribery case. *The New York Times*, p. 6.

Barnes, B., Yen, D., & Zhou, L. (2011). Investigating guanxi dimensions and relationship outcomes: Insights from Sino-Anglo business relationships. *Industrial Marketing Management*, 510–521.

Bauer, J., & Bell, D. (1999). *The East Asian challenge for human rights*. New York: Cambridge University Press.

BBC. (2012, March 29). *Apple's Tim Cook visits Foxconn China factory*. Retrieved March 13, 2020, from www.bbc.com/news/technology-17553296

BBC Monitoring Asia. (2005, May 21). US firm fined 4.8m dollars for bribing Chinese hospitals.

Beam, C. (2020, July 26). The NBA's jam. *The Wire China*, p. 1.

Bennet, J. (2020, May 11). *Trump walks out of press conference after altercation with female reporters*. Retrieved from https://www.business-standard.com/article/international/trump-ends-press-conference-after-altercation-with-two-women-reporters-120051200208_1.html

Berger, R., Herstein, R., Silbiger, A., & Barnes, B. (2015). Can guanxi be created in Sino–Western relationships? An assessment of Western firms trading with China using the GRX scale. *Industrial Marketing Management*, 166–174.

Bian, J. (2019). *Guanxi: How China works*. Medford, MA: Polity Press.

Buderi, R., & Huang, G. (2006). *Guanxi: The art of relationships*. New York: Simon and Schuster.

Choudhury, S. R. (2019, September 9). Apple denies claims it broke Chinese labor laws in iPhone factory. *CNBC Tech*. Retrieved July 22, 2020, from www.cnbc.com/2019/09/09/apple-appl-claims-it-broke-china-labor-laws-at-iphone-factory-mostly-false.html

D'Agostino, F. (2019). Contemporary approaches to the social contract. In *Stanford encyclopedia of philosophy*. Stanford: Stanford University Press.

De Menthe, B. L. (2013). *The Chinese way in business*. North Clarendon, VT: Tuttle.

Donaldson, T. (1989). *The ethics of international business*. New York: Oxford University Press.

Donaldson, T. (1996). Values in tension: Business away from home. *Harard Business Review*. Retrieved June 19, 2020, from https://hbr.org/1996/09/values-in-tension-ethics-away-from-home

Donaldson, T., & Dunfee, T. W. (1999). *Ties that bind: A social contracts approach to business ethics.* Boston: Harvard Business School Press.

Dreyer, M. (2019, October 10). China NBA: How one tweet derailed the NBA's China game plan. *BBC News.*

The Economist. (2007, August 6). Dirty dealing: Despite a clampdown, corruption remains a formidable problem, p. 55.

The Economist. (2010, May 29). Light and death; suicides at Foxconn. Retrieved from https://link-gale-com.libproxy.scu.edu/apps/doc/A228148111/STND?u=sant38536&sid=STND&xid=07e325df

Feldman, S. P. (2013). *Trouble in the middle.* New York: Routledge.

Feng, C. (2005, December 23). China declares war on business bribery. *Xinhua.* Retrieved from http://english.gov.cn/2005-12/23/content_135948.htm

Fred Bergsten, C. (2006). *China: The balance sheet.* New York: Public Affairs.

Friedman, M. (1970, September 13). The social responsibility of business is to increase its profits. *The New York Times*, p. 6.

Gurman, M. (2019, September 8). Apple, Foxconn broke a Chinese labor law to build latest iPhones. *Bloomberg News.* Retrieved July 20, 2020, from www.bloomberg.com/news/articles/2019-09-09/apple-foxconn-broke-a-chinese-labor-law-for-iphone-production

Hofstede, G., Hofstede, G., & Minkoc, M. (2010). *Cultures and organizations: Software of the mind.* New York: McGraw Hill.

Hsieh, N. H. (2015). Should business have human rights obligations? *Journal of Human Rights*, 218–236.

Hupert, A. (2014, April 25). *10 common China negotiating mistakes: A survival guide for front line negotiators and team leaders* (Kindle ed.). Hong Kong: China Solved.

Ihara, C. (2004). Are individual rights necessary? A Confucian perspective. In K. L. Shun & D. Wong (Eds.), *Confucian ethics* (pp. 11–30). New York: Cambridge University Press.

Ivanhoe, P. J., & Van Norden, B. W. (2005). *Readings in classical Chinese philosophy* (P. J. Ivanhoe & B. W. Van Norden, Trans.). Indianapolis: Hackett.

Kamm, J. (2020, April 11). Author Interview.

Kanematsu, Y. (2017, July 13). Foxconn, Apple and the partnership that changed the tech sector. *Nikkei Asian Review.* Retrieved from https://asia.nikkei.com/magazine/20170713/On-the-Cover/Foxconn-Apple-and-the-partnership-that-changed-the-tech-sector

Kent, A. (1993). *Between freedom and subsistence*. Hong Kong: Oxford University Press.

The New York Times Editorial Board. (2019, October 7). How a Tweet put the NBA in hot water in China. *The New York Times*, p. 1.

Nolan, J. (2011). Good guanxi and bad guanxi: Western bankers and the role of network. *The International Journal of Human Resource Management*, 3357–3372.

Ozanian, M. (2018, February 26). Mark Tatum talks about the NBA's enormous success in China and its impact on team values. *Forbes*.

Paine, L. S. (2002). *Value shift*. New York: McGraw Hill.

Pearce, J., & Robinson, R. (2000). Cultivating Guanxi as a foreign investor strategy. *Business Horizons*, 31–38.

Rosen, D. (1999). *Behind the open door: Foreign enterprises in the Chinese marketplace*. Washington, DC: Institute for International Economics.

Rothlin, S., & McCann, D. (2015). *International business ethics: Focus on China*. Berlin: Springer.

Santoro, M. (2000). *Profits and principles*. Ithaca, NY: Cornell University Press.

Santoro, M. (2003). Beyond codes of conduct and monitoring: An organizational integrity approach to global labor practices. *Human Rights Quarterly*, 407–424.

Santoro, M. (2009). *China 2020: How Western business can—and should—influence social and political change in the coming decade*. New York: Cornell University Press.

Santoro, M. (2015). Business and human rights in historical perspective. *Journal of Human Rights*, 155–161.

Saxon, M. (2006). *An American's guide to doing business in China: Negotiating contracts and agreements; understanding culture and customs; marketing products and services paperback*. Avon, MA: Adams Media.

Schoenberger, K. (1998, April 20). Has Levi Strauss sold out in China? *Los Angeles Times*, p. 1.

Stone, B. (2020, April 19). Author Interview. (M. Santoro, Interviewer).

Tsai, J. (2019, October 6). *Open letter*. Retrieved from https://bleacherreport.com/articles/2856027-nets-owner-joe-tsai-writes-open-letter-to-nba-fans-after-daryl-morey-china-tweet

United Nations. (2011a). *Principle 11*. Geneva: Author.

United Nations. (2011b). *Principle 13b*. Geneva: Author.

Verstappen, S. (2015). *Chinese business etiquette*. Berkeley: Stone Bridge Press.

Vincent, J. (2016, May 6). Tim Cook reportedly traveling to China following closure of Apple's online stores. *The Verge*. Retrieved July 22, 2020, from www.theverge.com/2016/5/6/11606412/apple-china-books-movies-tim-cook-visit

Wang, C., & Zhan, Y. (2010, May 25). 11 consecutive suicides in Foxconn, government got. *Xinhua News Online*.

Wettstein, F. (2009). *Multinational corporations and global justice: Human rights obligations of a quasi-governmental institution*. Stanford: Stanford University Press.

Woetzel, J., & Towson, J. (2017). *The 1-hour China book*. Cayman Islands: Towson Group.

Yen, D., Barnes, B., & Wang, C. (2011). The measurement of guanxi: Introducing the GRX scale. *Industrial Marketing Management*, 97–108.

5

BEYOND FACE AND *GUĀNXI*

Foundational normative concepts and values of traditional Chinese ethics

Our discussion to this point has been on an elementary level—we might call it the "introductory course" in traditional Chinese ethics. Learning and applying the fundamentals of face and guānxi constitute only the most basic level of ethical fluency required to operate effectively in China. For many business executives, Chapters 2–4 may be as far as you want to go and perhaps as far as you need to go. However, if you are operating and thinking only at that level, you are still a stranger in a strange land, albeit one who can communicate and function with some effectiveness. For those who want to or need to function at a deeper level of understanding, this chapter is closer to an "intermediate course" in which we pull aside the curtain to reveal what is going on behind the Ethical Triad, Ethical Agility, face, and guānxi. In this chapter, we examine five normative concepts that distinguish ethical from unethical behavior within relationships: Xiào (孝)/Piety or Hierarchy, Lǐ (禮)/Propriety, Zhì (智)/Wisdom, Yì (義)/Uprightness, and Rén (仁)/Humaneness. Because such issues are of concern to many Westerners, we give consideration to the intersection of these concepts with

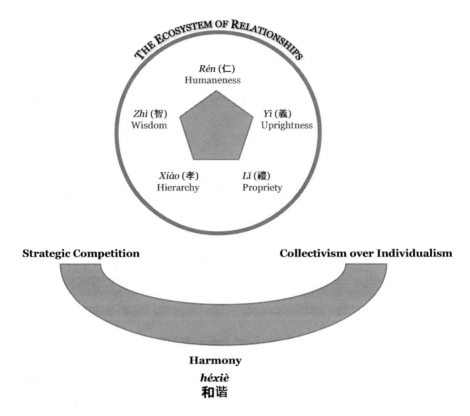

Figure 5.1 Five normative concepts of relationships and three foundational values of Chinese ethics

gender as well as LGBTQ+ citizens within China. We then describe three foundational values—harmony, strategic competition, and collectivism over individualism—that undergird not just relationships, but Chinese ethics, etiquette, society, and culture more broadly. The general framework we outline in this chapter is illustrated in Figure 5.1.

As we dive more deeply into details of Chinese ethics we will come to appreciate two essential verities that are applicable to every attempt to compare and reconcile different systems of ethics. First, we will find that the traditional Chinese system of ethics is complete in itself and uniquely defines and governs relations among persons, families, and groups in a way that is elementally different in nature to the ethical and religious precepts predominating in the West. At the same time, whatever their respective metaphysical, epistemological, or religious origins might be, there is, at the end of the day, a certain unity of purpose for all systems of ethics that would govern human interaction and social construction. It would take us very far afield to speculate on the question of whether it is possible to discern commonalities or achieve a synthesis of every major ethical system into one "global ethics."[16] However, in this chapter we will, when possible, point out some of the more plausible points of connection between Chinese and Western approaches to ethics. Moreover, because of the great number of topics covered, instead of case studies at the end of the chapter, we will in each instance immediately describe ways the concepts can be put into practice, sometimes drawing on our discussions in previous chapters.

5.1 Five normative concepts guiding the Chinese ecosystem of relationships

A central theme of this book has been the importance of relationships—family, clan, regional, ethnic, and so on—which integrate with both personal and business interactions. Relationships define how much ethical, etiquette, personal, and business consideration a person deserves and expects from you, and vice-versa. The closer and more personal the relationship—which may also be a business relationship—the more one owes, but also the more one is owed in return. This was the notion of increasing ethical consideration or concern as relationships deepen. While, as we have noted, Western ethical precepts in many cases would caution against relationship-based ethics as unfair nepotism or, worse yet, corrupt cronyism, relationship-based ethics are not entirely foreign in the West. A Western parallel of the Chinese principle that relationships are an organizing ethical phenomenon can be found as far back as the Hebrew Bible (a.k.a., "Old Testament"). The ancient Hebrew relationship with the deity meant that the Ten Commandments applied to Hebrews as a group and not, as is sometimes thought nowadays, to all people universally, which is a later Christian belief. This explains why there is an apparent tension surrounding the commandment "you shall not murder" (often translated as "kill," but that is a misleading translation of the

16 Two excellent comparative works on Chinese and Western philosophy, including ethics, are Angle and Slote (2013) and Van Norden (2007). For a thoroughgoing and thoughtful attempt to reconcile Islam, Hinduism, and Christianity, see Kung, Von Stietencron, and Van Ess (1993).

Hebrew root r-ts-ch, or רצח, which is a legal concept, not just a biological one). The deity commands Hebrews to kill Philistines by the hundreds, which may seem like a paradox. However, the paradox dissolves when one takes the view that, because of the divine covenant, those commandments apply to and within Hebrew society, not to outsiders. One's status as Hebrew thus makes a difference to the legal and moral status one deserves and receives. Though a subject of debate among moral philosophers, preference for one's family or clan is a widespread fact of everyday moral life in the West. However, in China and arguably much of Asia, relationship-based ethics are more the norm than the exception they are in the West (Chinn, 2020).

Beyond understanding that relationships constitute an important ethical touchstone, it is also important to appreciate that the manner in which one behaves in various relationships is governed by a set of normative concepts. Thus far we have only looked at the connection between relationships and ethics monochromatically as a function of relative strength or closeness. We will now, however, consider five normative concepts that distinguish ethical from unethical behavior within relationships. These concepts are heavily influenced by Confucianism. Although Confucianism does not fully define Chinese ethics, culture, behavior, and mindsets, it does play an outsized role in guiding proper behavior within relationships, in part because of the Confucian emphasis on the family and the relationships it contains as the basic organizing social unit.

5.1.1 Xiào (孝)/Hierarchy

First, and deeply Interconnected with Chinese concepts of relationships, is the notion of xiào (孝), which is often translated as "piety" or "filial piety," but as those terms have religious connotations in the West, xiào is better translated as "hierarchy" in the context of business. Many relationships, personal and professional, involve hierarchical differences between the people in the relationship—for example, older/younger, senior/junior, superior/subordinate, higher-ranking/lower-ranking, and so on. Even among friend-friend relationships, an older or more professionally established friend might typically be treated with some additional deference by a younger or less-established friend, just on that account. Traditionally, Confucianism posits five fundamental relationships: ruler-subject, father-son, husband-wife, older brother-younger brother, friend-friend. In Chinese and other cultures influenced by Confucianism, these relationships are often thought of as a kind of blueprint for relationships generally, such that all personal-business relationships map to greater or lesser degree onto one of these five basic ones.

This principle of hierarchy in relationships is taken to extend through pretty much every aspect of Chinese culture and everyday life, extending out from family relationships to include those in business and government. Fundamentally, superiors are to behave benevolently towards subordinates, guiding them with wisdom, while subordinates are to behave respectfully and loyally towards superiors. Because hierarchy operates within relationships, and because this extends throughout daily life in Chinese culture contexts including business, the widespread Western principle to treat everyone the same does not make sense. To Chinese perspectives, acting that way is disrespectful of the relationships (especially close ones) and hierarchies that are present in every context, and people who have Awareness know this. Books on business etiquette in China often include great detail on certain clues of social hierarchy in Chinese culture contexts, especially on the mainland. These include which brand of cigarettes one should smoke, what brands and quality of alcohol one should order at banquets, what watch one should wear, and so on. We leave it to books focused more closely on those clues to lay out their subtleties.[17] The broad practical takeaway here is to understand that equality and sameness of treatment are not guiding principles of how one interacts with others in Chinese culture contexts. Instead, one must behave respectfully—as superior, subordinate, or in some cases equals—by acting within the established system of hierarchical relationships governed by *xiào*.

5.1.2 Lǐ (禮)/Propriety

A second principle is lǐ (禮), sometimes itself translated as "principle" or "ritual," but also often translated as "good form, formality, etiquette" (Kroll, 2017, p. 261). For the purposes of business, lǐ is better translated as "propriety" in the sense of commonly shared guidelines of what counts as

---

17   For extended detailed discussions see, e.g., Hu et al. (2010), De Menthe (2013), Collinsworth (2014), and Verstappen (2015).

appropriate behavior in any given situation.[18] Lǐ applies to a wide range of situations, from momentary everyday events—such as greeting friends versus strangers, how to show respect to a superior or higher-ranking person, how to treat a subordinate, and so on—to more momentous events such as banquets, public speeches, or meeting a Chinese minister to negotiate a business deal. That lǐ encompasses all of these is one reason why we introduced Interconnectedness in Chapter 2. Not only are ethics and etiquette not clearly conceptually distinguished, but moreover in lǐ there is a background belief that the same body of guidelines and norms applies to both—to big behaviors and small, momentous and everyday. This is a further reason why foreign businesses and business executives operating in China need to recognize that the "basics" of politeness are not a "nice to have" but are integral to ethical behavior by their connection to showing respect, preserving face, and participating in guānxi networks. If you fail to exhibit rudimentary understanding of lǐ, then you make yourself an outsider. As should be clear from our discussions of relationships as well as Chapters 2 through 4, if you render yourself an outsider, as a result you become "fair game," ethically speaking, and deserve minimal ethical consideration (Mark Zuckerberg, for example). Furthermore, instead of being a friend and thereby someone to cooperate with, you become someone with whom to strategically compete (as we elaborate in the next section).

A specific example of lǐ guidelines at work in everyday business situations is the importance of what we will call "quietude," especially in terms of expressing confidence in the workplace. A proverb sums it up succinctly: "confidence is quiet, insecurity is loud." Though this line is sometimes heard in both the East and the West, in Chinese culture contexts bluster and overt confidence are considered low, base, and even "barbaric." Except sometimes when talking to an underling, someone who is glib, bossy, or blustery is signaling that they do not have real power or influence. A persistent theme in the Confucian *Analects* is that people who are glib or showy, who talk too quickly, who emphasize profit over propriety, and whose actions do not measure up to their words, deserve dire criticism and mistrust (*Analects* 1:3, 3:1, 4:5, 4:9, 4:12, 4:16, 7:12). These are values that many Westerners

---

18   If at any point the reader becomes concerned or even skeptical that so many terms may be used to translate a single Chinese word, we point out how many words it would take to accurately translate English "cool" into other languages—most often, "cool" itself is used, untranslated.

uphold, so they should be familiar. However, many Western—and especially American—businesspeople are taught to, and rewarded for, being assertive and outwardly confident. (This is notwithstanding the double-standard that many women face who are labeled "bossy" or worse for exactly the same behavior.) That training, and resultant behaviors, are highly counterproductive in Chinese and many other East-Asian culture contexts.[19]

Quietude also helps explain an observation about understatement that is sometimes made by Western businesspeople working not just in China but elsewhere in East Asia. The observation is that, to Western perspectives, many East Asian businesspeople do not say what they mean. For example, as discussed in Chapter 2, to say "no" (as in, "no, we would not be able to make that deadline") erodes the face of the person to whom you say "no." As a result, whether or not "no" is the actual answer, to say so outright is considered very rude. Instead, as experienced China-hands know, "it would be difficult" means "no," while "maybe" means "probably not." Similarly, if someone is asked if they know or understand something, "I've studied it a bit" can mean "I am quite knowledgeable" and "I have some experience" can mean "I'm an expert." Quietude is also operating beneath the surface in our discussion of Hank Paulson's meeting with Zhu Rongji in Chapter 2: Paulson was not waiting to hear "yes," he was waiting to hear "we hope to cooperate with you" (Paulson, 2015, p. 12). Once one has Awareness of this aspect of Chinese culture, it is fairly clear what the person meant.

We have tried to avoid too many predictions, in part because of how difficult China has proven to predict, but here we suspect that as the world becomes increasingly global and as the internet generation (eventually) comes to power in China, businesspeople will be able to meet on more of a middle-ground in terms of quietude, at least as regards assertiveness and modesty, so that such misunderstandings may become less common. Increasingly, Chinese businesspeople may become more familiar and perhaps comfortable with relatively assertive cultures to the point where assertiveness may

19 This difference in how confidence is expressed is not unique to China-West divides, but sometimes also occurs within Western culture contexts, such as between Dutch and American businesspeople in interviews. To Dutch perspectives, Americans oversell themselves, while to American perspectives Dutch interviewees undersell themselves. When businesspeople are unaware of these differences, Dutch interviewees come across as under-qualified, while American hires are perceived as under-delivering (Hofstede, Hofstede, & Minkov, 2010, p. 136).

become less of an excuse to write off blustery foreigners. In the meantime, though, such foreigners have the opportunity to become increasingly global and thereby more effective in China by practicing modesty in the presence of their Chinese counterparts.

5.1.3 Zhì (智)/Wisdom

A third normative concept governing relationships is zhì (智), which is often translated as "understanding," "insight," or better for our purposes, "wisdom." Wisdom, zhì, is essentially a sense of good judgment as regards ethics and etiquette, which is acquired by cultural learning plus life experience. Having wisdom means being able to recognize not just the situations that have ethical implications and consequences, but to anticipate the implications and consequences of the particular choices and decisions one makes. Wisdom is what allowed Confucius to recognize that he needed to give different advice to students of differing temperaments in order to achieve positive outcomes for those students (*Analects* 11:22). The importance of wisdom was operating beneath the surface of Awareness, introduced in Chapter 2. Having Awareness, being "tuned into" subtle but important aspects of the various situations in which we find ourselves is important for identifying the etiquette and ethical cues that let us figure out how to behave correctly in Chinese culture contexts. Both the identifying and the figuring-out are encompassed by wisdom. Importantly, wisdom is neither exclusively Confucian nor exclusively Chinese—many Daoists could agree that wisdom is a virtue, and many ethical traditions, Eastern and Western, hold that a carefully-trained sense of moral judgment is important for behaving ethically (Van Norden, 2007). What is important to the ecosystem of relationships is that because the ecosystem is large and involves many subtleties, one must be able to perceive those subtleties in order to discern how to act properly. For example, a wise person accurately and quickly perceives the relationships and hierarchies operating in any particular situation and can then discern how to act in light of that understanding.

One business application of wisdom that is familiar to many people who have spent time in East-Asian culture contexts is gift-giving as it relates to maintaining relationships, including acknowledging successful negotiations and business deals. Not just brute knowledge of the situation, but insight—wisdom—is needed to navigate these situations. On the one hand, there is an expectation of gift-giving, which traditionally holds that bigger, more valuable gifts are exchanged to acknowledge bigger deals, as well as more senior people. Not participating in this practice erodes face for Chinese counterparts, can sabotage deals, and in many cases has been perceived by Westerners as reducing the competitiveness of Western firms in China. Yet, on the other hand, home-country laws, company policy, or both, restrict or can even eliminate the ability to give appropriate gifts. Wisdom is how the ethically cultivated person sees through the dilemma and acts well. A wise Western businessperson can commiserate with their Chinese partner that home-country restrictions are an unfortunate example of differing legal and moral standards, and can then give a gift consistent with those restrictions along with a carefully-written note acknowledging that the gift is inadequate while extolling their respect for the Chinese partner and their ongoing cooperation (Bian, 2019).

5.1.4 Yì (義)/Uprightness

A fourth normative concept governing relationships is *yì* (義), which is often translated as "righteousness" but that has religious connotations for many Westerners, so as regards business a better translation is "uprightness." The original idea of uprightness, *yì*, was dutifulness with regard to the responsibilities acknowledged as appropriate within one's "we" group and its relationships; for instance, the responsibility of a child to a father outstripping responsibilities to authorities in the sheep-story (Kroll, 2017, p. 550). In more depth, uprightness means acting in accordance with *xiào*, *lǐ*, and *zhì*—that is, actually behaving ethically, even when it may be difficult or inconvenient to do so. No matter one's initial framework in ethics, whether it be Chinese or Western, Confucian or Aristotelian, doing the right thing sometimes requires the moral courage to uphold both ethical and etiquette ideals even when in the face of adversity or risk. This quality is uprightness. Uprightness also relates to face and *guānxi*: fulfilling one's duties within one's reciprocal relationships (*guānxi*) and promoting another person's face can sometimes come at a cost, or at least risk, to you.

A familiar business example involving uprightness, *yì*, would be when you are ordered to do something illegal (like ignore an accounting irregularity or fudge numbers in advance of a quarterly report), or you observe something problematic such as "bad" *guānxi* in the form of excessive nepotism or bribery. As we discussed in connection with supply-chain problems, "calling out" someone, even when justified in principle, is typically counterproductive in Chinese culture contexts. Not only can it slow down problem-solving, but it can introduce risk to you, your company, customers, and so on. One way that can happen is that, as a Chinese counterpart moves to save their own face (perhaps by breaking ties, suddenly finding a "problem" with a contract, or even flinging counter-accusations), and as they mobilize their *guānxi* networks to reduce any professional damage to them, you may come under suspicion and find yourself on the defense, in addition to wasting time while the problematic behavior continues. Such problems are much more likely to be addressed, and you can maintain uprightness, *yì*, by not speaking out publicly about your suspicions of unethical or illegal practice, and instead privately speaking up about your concerns. In both China and the West, it is often difficult to know whom to talk to, but if you have cultivated relationships, you will have them available as a resource, both for advice on how to proceed as well as to navigate your way to having the problem addressed. By working quickly in private through close connections you and your firm have, you dramatically increase the chances of a successful resolution while minimizing the chance of blowback to you. (Sample scripts for how such difficult conversations might go are scattered throughout Chapters 2–4.)

5.1.5 Rén (仁)/Humaneness

A fifth and final normative concept governing relationships is rén (仁), often translated as "benevolence" or "humaneness." In different ways, both are apt.[20] On the one hand, humaneness can be understood as an all-encompassing principle, in the sense that the more ethically cultivated a person you are, the more fully you treat yourself and others humanely (Shun, 2002). This means that in interactions with others, you consistently practice the values scattered throughout this book but especially in this section—hierarchy, wisdom, propriety, and uprightness (Yu, Tao, & Ivanhoe, 2009). To be truly humane is to be all of those things. Our framework of

---

20 The Confucian ideal of rén (仁) governs behavior within relationships, but it is not constrained only to relationships. As we discuss, part of the concept is an all-encompassing notion of humaneness, or being a good person. However, that level of depth we leave for philosophy seminars—for discussion, see for example Hall and Ames (1987, pp. 110–130).

Context-First, Interconnectedness, Awareness, and the ability to apply those, Agility, is designed to show Western mindsets how to become fluid enough to not only understand but also behave in accordance with this comprehensive principle of humaneness (rén).

A narrower, but equally accurate, notion of rén consists in behaving benevolently towards those within one's network of relationships, especially towards those who are your equals, juniors, and subordinates. As ever, the exact behavior that constitutes benevolence depends on hierarchy and the exact nature of the relationship (closeness, duration, rank in the firm, and so on). Concrete specifics of how to behave within relationships also depend on the preceding principles discussed in this chapter: does one understand and practice the common guidelines for proper behavior, including etiquette (lǐ); does one show the respect and deference to one's superiors while showing leadership towards one's juniors (xiào); does one do what is ethically required even when it is inconvenient to oneself (yì); and does one exhibit the insight needed to appropriately apply these principles to the particular situations in which one finds oneself (zhì)?

Although the foregoing list of normative concepts governing relationships is different from a comparable list of Western principles, there is nonetheless significant overlap. A standard list of Western ethical principles might start: integrity, honesty, respect, loyalty, wisdom, benevolence, compassion, justice, and so on. The Chinese list began: hierarchy, propriety, wisdom, uprightness, and humaneness. Superficially, some of these words are different, but the concepts intersect. Wisdom, the ability to have not just understanding but knowing where and how to apply it, appears on both lists. Whereas in the West we might talk about integrity to describe standing up for what is right in the face of obstacles, in Chinese contexts we talk about uprightness (yì). Whereas in Western contexts we might talk about respect and loyalty to describe how we should behave towards our superiors, our departments, our companies, and even our countries, in Chinese contexts we talk about hierarchy or "filial piety" (xiào). Whereas in the West we might talk about benevolence, treating others well, or engaging in social responsibility, in Chinese contexts we would talk about humaneness (rén) both in general and specifically towards those with whom we, and our organizations, have relationships.

It is also worth stressing that even though "respect" does not appear overtly on the Chinese list, it is operating behind some of the principles, especially hierarchy (*xiào*) and propriety (*lǐ*), and is also crucial to both face as well as *guānxi*. Chinese and Western perspectives alike prioritize showing respect. At its foundations, the concept is the same East to West—the difference is that one *shows* respect differently in differing cultural contexts. In Chinese culture contexts—and others around the globe—showing respect is not just about who speaks in what order, who leads a discussion, or who defers to whom. As one longtime traveler to East Asia put it,

> whenever people acknowledge the history and culture of China (or Korea) while in these countries and show some familiarity with the customs, history, and beliefs, it makes working together easier and more effective. Some Westerners need to understand that respect is much more than a matter of not violating another's rights; it also includes showing interest in and appreciation of their distinctive way of life . . . it includes things that are about peoples and not just persons.
>
> (Ivanhoe, Interview, 2020)

5.2 Gender and LGBTQ+ rights, and Confucian ethics

Before moving on to the next section, we must address what for some readers will seem like an elephant in the room: how these five normative concepts and the societies influenced by them, by Confucianism, relate to the statuses of women and LGBTQ+ people. Though Confucianism is not the only enduring cultural influence in China, it remains highly influential there, throughout much of East Asia including Japan and South Korea, as well as in Vietnam and associated diasporas (Rozman, 1991). Its ideas therefore influence the day-to-day lives, and commerce, of at least one-fifth the world's population (US Census Bureau, 2020). As we have discussed, traditional transmissionism is a core idea of Confucianism—this is the idea that harmonious societies and the process of ethical cultivation both entail the transmission of certain traditions and traditional ideals. Regarding parents in particular, such traditions demand tremendous deference and obedience. This is implied by *xiào* (hierarchy) as applied to parent-child relationships, and is evident in many famous Confucian quotations, for example:

> In serving your parents you may gently remonstrate with them. However, once it becomes apparent that they have not taken your

criticism to heart you should be respectful and not oppose them, and follow their lead diligently without resentment.

(Ivanhoe & Van Norden, 2005, p. 12)

Because of its emphasis on transmitting traditions, including within families, Confucianism therefore is, to significant degree, a socially conservative philosophy.

As part of its social conservatism, Confucianism is widely understood as advocating very traditional gender-roles and -norms across the societies it has influenced (Grant, 2008, Koh, 2008). It is referenced not only as an explanation but also as a justification for why these norms persist so strongly, including by China's most famous woman scholar, Ban Zhao, who has been called simultaneously feminist and anti-feminist (Zhao, 1900, Yang, 2016). Historically, Confucian societies viewed women with greater honor and respect than many have supposed (Swann, 1994), and following the Communist revolution, many barriers to women working outside the home and having public professional lives were dramatically reduced. However, while there is variation depending on region and socioeconomic status, it is common in China today for women to have more responsibility than power in family life (Liu, 1994). In the workplace, top positions in government and many sectors of business continue to be male-dominated (Flannery, 2013). As usual, however, the issue is nuanced: China's situation is different than many Western countries where girls and women outnumber men and boys, yet gender imbalance persists in many sectors of industry. By contrast, gender imbalance in China starts at birth, with significantly more boys born than girls, partly as a result of cultural preferences for boys that go back into antiquity and that were made more acute by the one-child policy of the late 20th century (Xie, 1994, BBC, 2010, Reuters, 2015). Confucianism is no doubt complicit in explaining the perpetuation of these realities, but several factors continue to reduce equity in the personal and professional lives of women in China today.

Another outgrowth of Confucian-influenced traditionalism about gender-roles and families is a decisively hetero-normic notion of the family according to which a—or perhaps the—main purpose of family is for male-female couples to marry and have children (preferably, to many Chinese parents, boys) (Rofel, 2007, pp. 97–102). Homosexuality was decriminalized in China in 1997, and removed from the official list of mental illnesses in

2001 (Associated Press, 2001, Sheehan, 2017a). These are far from the earliest dates for such events among nations around the world, but it is notable that there remain many nations where simply being gay or trans remains a crime, in some cases punishable by death. In China, despite decriminalization, traditional ideals yet again exert considerable influence on contemporary thought and behavior. For example, homosexual couples living together continue to be harassed and even prosecuted, not under anti-gay laws, but under public nuisance laws (Rofel, 2007, pp. 85–110). Paralleling Xie Feng's allusion to Confucius in his op-ed about China's handling of COVID-19, the scholar Fang Xudong quoted Mencius in support of his claim that the Confucian duty to produce children outstrips one's own need for happiness, while simultaneously (and implausibly, in his case) asserting "Confucians don't have any discrimination against homosexual people" (方旭东, 2015, Sheehan, 2017b). Confucianism and Confucian ethics are therefore one of many strains of thought that have had enduring and decidedly not unilaterally positive influences on the lived experiences of LGBTQ+ people and women, including in the workplace.

It is not clear how things are most likely to go for LGBTQ+ people and women in the foreseeable future in China. At various times and under various regimes, traditional strains of thought have been touted, denounced, or simply twisted to the purposes of various leaders by way of legitimizing their initiatives, especially in the 20th and early 21st centuries (Nylan & Wilson, 2010, pp. 192–246). International awareness of, and pressure towards equal protection have been raised, for example by the #metoo movement and by increasingly many countries legalizing same-sex marriage. Perhaps Fang Xudong was surprised when the Confucian canon was cited in support of same-sex marriage in the US Supreme Court's decision on *Obergefell v. Hodges*, though that reference was ridiculed by Justice Scalia in a note to the dissenting opinion as "mystical aphorisms of the fortune cookie" (Van Norden, 2015).

On the one hand, there are grounds for pessimism, as patriarchy and hetero-normativity are arguably hard-wired into influential traditional Chinese views on family relationships and the norms governing them— another Chinese scholar Zeng Yi publicly called same-sex marriage an "anti-human crime" (Tsoi-lai, 2015). Furthermore, a cultural emphasis on social harmony serves to hold back many women and LGBTQ+ people in public and the workplace, partly because it reinforces the desire not to "stand out" (Rofel, 2007). Yet, on the other hand, there are grounds for reasonable optimism—slowly but surely the internet generation will come into power in China. Though there is significant variation across socioeconomic classes, many women report greater equity of treatment, especially as China's first women astronauts took to space (O'Sullivan, 2012). A 2014 survey by *The Chinese Journal of Human Sexuality* indicated that nearly 85 percent of Chinese people already supported same-sex marriage (Tsoi-lai, 2015). Alibaba has officially endorsed same-sex marriage, and together with Chinese LGBTQ+- oriented dating app Blued, has sponsored LGBTQ+ destination weddings outside China (Sheehan, 2017a). Change, therefore, is in the air though it seems most likely to be slow if pursued from within Chinese frameworks.

In the West, progress on these issues is often made by appeal to human and legal rights, but as we have discussed, bringing rights into the conversation tends to muddy debates in Chinese culture contexts. This is in large part because doing so introduces an additional controversy (rights) to the conversation about women's and LGBTQ+ status. In sum, as people continue to suffer indignity and inequity, it is probably too soon to tell, but there seems to be growing support for expanding Chinese notions of social harmony in the coming years and decades that could improve conditions considerably (Sheehan, 2017b).

5.3 Beyond relationships—three grounding values of Chinese ethics

In the West, we might start a list of ground-level ethical values like this: promoting justice and freedom; maximizing happiness and other goods; treating others not just as means to our own ends but as ends in themselves; acting in ways we would want others to act; leading a virtuous life at work and at home; etc. Lynn Sharp Paine offers a more specific list of such values, which also displays Western Rule-First thinking: "do right, be honest, be fair, keep promises, obey the spirit of the law" (Paine, 2002). However, if we are to do that for Chinese approaches to ethics, the list starts differently: promoting harmony; strategic competition; and collectivism over individualism. Because of Interconnectedness, these values are not exclusively ethical, and at first may not sound to Western ears like values at all, yet they guide everyday ethics, etiquette, society, and culture. These values, therefore, are less directly connected to the ecosystem of relationships, but help define the broader ethical-cultural landscape (of which relationships are a central part).

5.3.1 Harmony

The first, and arguably the most important, foundational value in traditional Chinese ethics is harmony, often translated as héxiè (和谐). At the most elemental level, harmony is what ethical thought and behavior aim to achieve. The ethically cultivated person lives in harmony, not only with themselves, but also with those surrounding them, and even the environment (Zhuangzi, 2009, pp. 7–8, Xunzi, 1999, pp. 208–261). Within Chinese philosophy, traditions that otherwise disagree on very many things—for example, Confucianism and Daoism—nonetheless agree on the importance of achieving harmony in various forms. The cultivated person does not strive to stand out, does not openly gather prestige for themselves, and does not openly strive to overcome or defeat competitors. Such behavior is considered rather gross and barbaric. For example, disruption, that core value of many Western technology firms, is not an overt value in China, meaning that while disruption certainly occurs in China, overt disruptiveness is viewed as uncouth and uncivilized behavior. A well-known proverb sums up this mindset succinctly: "the nail that sticks out gets hammered down." According to this mindset, success is not associated with overt success, excellence, or standing out (as in Aristotelian ethics, for example), but rather with fitting in and participating seamlessly within one's relationships, guānxi networks, co-workers, family, institutions, and society more broadly.

One way to appreciate the centrality of harmony in traditional Chinese culture is to consider its relationship to paradox, a common cultural-philosophical stumbling block for many Westerners living and doing business in China. Chinese perspectives, in general, tend to be more tolerant of paradoxes than common Western ones. Starting in Ancient Greece, but especially since the Enlightenment—which came with the advent of modern science and the brazen hope that rational humanistic thought could solve or resolve nearly every human problem—a widespread Western perspective on paradox is that it is to be studied, analyzed, and ultimately resolved or if not, at least explained away. By contrast, to many Chinese perspectives, a paradox is viewed less as a problem that must be solved, or resolved, than as a discovery or even just a fact of life. Acceptance of paradox is a way of preserving overall harmony where circumstances and events might seem discordant to many Westerners.

There are myriad examples of apparent paradoxes encountered by Western business executives doing business in China. One concerns Chinese views of time. One the one hand, Chinese counterparts can seem to be endlessly patient. As Chinese proverb has it: "time is the only thing that's free." Of course, this is in direct opposition to the common Western (perhaps especially American) aphorism: "time is money." Businesspeople in situations like that of The Hurried Executive in Chapter 2 often report frustration that Chinese counterparts seem to be waiting out negotiations rather than trying to get a deal done. This is, in part, to test out and to get to know potential business partners better. However, it can also be a negotiating tactic used to force the hand of Westerners who feel the pressure of time more acutely and will eventually accept a deal that is less favorable to them and their firms—a smart move from Chinese perspectives (we go into more detail in the next section). At the same time, however, other things happen very quickly in China, including research and development of tech, as well as construction in cities. We propose looking at it this way: some things happen slowly because it takes time to get to know people and one wants the most advantageous deal one can get for one's firm. Another reason is that lower-level folks often have neither the authority nor the inclination to make decisions for which they may be held accountable—typically, any proposal or decision has to "slinky" its way up, and then back down, the chain of command before action may be taken. As Hank Paulson noted, his counterparts were often slow to decide, but then quick to act. Additionally, one needs to be able to trust one's business partners since one cannot trust the government and legal system to avoid or resolve problems. Other things happen quickly because they are a matter of national pride and prestige (like AI research), or because they are a matter of desperate need, as millions of people continue to move from rural China to cities that have better work opportunities (like coastal construction). Awareness of what motivates Chinese government officials, businesspeople, and citizens helps us understand this paradox.

Another highly salient paradox is that of innovation versus traditionalism. When we were talking about IP in Chapter 2, we discussed how many Chinese businesspeople view IP losses as theft and as a serious problem, yet culturally speaking, it is not viewed to be as serious a problem as many Western businesspeople view it. We cited one book on the subject, which has a telling title: *To Steal a Book is an Elegant Offence*. In China there is, and has been for millennia, a widespread perception that older is better, that new ideas are not to be trusted, and that transmitting ideas is better than (overt) innovation and disruption. Confucius is quoted as having said "Following the proper way, I do not forge new paths; with confidence I cherish the ancients—in these respects I am comparable to our venerable Old Peng," a legendary storyteller and hence transmitter of ancient wisdom (Ames & Rosemont, 1999, p. 111). More recently, Zhou Enlai is often quoted as having said "it's too soon to tell" when asked in 1972 about the impact of the French Revolution. Though apparently arising from a misunderstanding in translation—he almost certainly interpreted the question as referring to the 1968 uprisings in Paris—the translation was allowed to stand, in part because such a remark is nonetheless consistent with Chinese perspectives on how long it can take for ideas to become established (Cowen, 2011). In China, old and established are a matter of millennia, not years or even centuries—culturally and politically speaking, neither three years nor 173 years is a long time in China. Yet, there is tremendous innovation happening in China, especially in AI and other areas of technology including social media platforms. How do these perspectives square with one another? Perhaps they do not—our message here is to highlight the almost-instinctive Western need for everything to make rational sense. Examining the situation closely reveals quite different motivations around technology development (national honor and prestige on the world stage, plus perhaps also the government's ability to maintain control of information), which are largely separate from a generalized tendency to prefer, take pride in, and trust the older over the newer. Yet again, both can be true.

5.3.2 *Strategic competition*

A second foundational value of Chinese ethics and culture is what we call "strategic competition." To Western ears this might not sound like a value. However, in part because of the emphasis on harmony, a basic moral instinct in Chinese ethics and culture is to avoid, or at least minimize, open conflict. At the same time, business, and life generally, involve competition—for access to resources, market share, lucrative contracts and partnerships, etc. The value is not that one ought to avoid competing per se, but rather this: given that one must compete anyway, the ethical way is to do so strategically so as to reduce disruptions to harmony. What defines strategy has been influenced by a variety of classic Chinese sources, but two of the most influential are the *Daodejing* and *The Art of War*. The latter is often misread by Westerners as a treatise on how to conduct war and win at all costs, but is in actuality a book about how to avoid warfare—specifically to avoid the destruction of people and resources, as well as the disruption of social harmony, that war creates. As the great General Cao Cao noted in his commentary on the *Art of War*, "the wise win before the fight, while the ignorant fight to win." The apparent tension between competition and harmony is yet another example of increased tolerance for paradoxes—this tension becomes less acute, however, when one realizes that part of the strategy is to minimize disruptions to social harmony while increasing one's own resources, maintaining face and *guānxi*, and so on. Such a strategic outlook emphasizes the "long game" and ultimate victory rather than immediate reward and prestige.

The importance and ubiquity of strategic competition in Chinese society and business is, as is often the case, largely a result of history. Resources have been scarce in China for a very long time—1,300 years ago during the golden age of the Tang Dynasty, the population exceeded 50 million, and its capital was the largest city in the world by population (Banister, 1992). For contrast, that time included the reign of Charlemagne in Europe, when the population of that entire continent is estimated to have been half that of China's yet Europe is twice the size by area of the Tang dynasty's greatest extent (Russell, 1972, pp. 25–71). During the 16th century under the Ming Dynasty, China's population surpassed 100 million, when all of Europe's surpassed 70 million (Champion & Aubin, 2020). Scarcity of resources is thus a long-standing cultural assumption in China. For these, among other socio-political and economic reasons, a foundational assumption has guided Chinese life and society for centuries: if someone is an outsider and not within your family, clan, or *guānxi* networks, then you are in strategic competition with them for resources. These resources have typically included water, food, land, and places to live—especially in cities—as well as access to government favor and recourse for wrongs done. In business, resources include opportunities such as increasing responsibility, promotions, and partnerships. To repeat: anyone who is not an insider is a presumed competitor.

As we discussed in previous chapters, this often leads to fundamental China–West misunderstandings in business. A typical Western mindset might come to the negotiating table looking for a partner with whom to make a deal that is mutually beneficial to both sides. Indeed, as we saw in Chapters 2-4, this is the appropriate rhetoric for those situations. But, to typical Chinese mindsets, that only makes sense among people already within their guānxi networks. Typical Chinese perspectives on the same activity of sitting down at the table are: you are looking to strike a deal advantageous to your firm, they are doing the same for their firm, and this process will not happen in a single sitting anyway. (Chapter 4 explained how to get past this situation, through understanding, time, and effort.)

Given this competitor-perspective on sitting down at the negotiating table, Western businesspeople are well-advised to learn and apply Chinese wisdom regarding strategic competition. Drawing from *The Art of War*, for example, such wisdom includes: (i) know yourself, in terms of strengths and weaknesses (including impatience, when compared with many Chinese perspectives on negotiation); (ii) know your enemy (who is at the table, what relationships are operating in the situation, which individuals ultimately make the decision, how will they perceive the prestige and title of the chief negotiator on your side, show them respect that they will recognize as increasing face, anticipate redirections and even misdirections, etc.); (iii) know the terrain (what are the background conditions of the negotiation, such as the political climate, relevant histories between the two firms, competing firms with whom the Chinese firm may be talking, how much time your leadership has given to make a deal, etc.); and (iv) mislead your competitor so that they cannot know you as well as you know them (appear more disorganized than you really are, do not fully reveal your negotiating strategy or approach right away, perhaps do not immediately reveal everything your firm is hoping to get out of the partnership, perhaps introduce your own redirections and misdirections, etc.) (Sunzi, 2011).

5.3.3 *Collectivism over individualism*

A third foundational value of traditional Chinese ethics, often discussed by sociologists, is "collectivism over individualism." Generally speaking, the emphasis in Chinese culture contexts is on the well-being and face of the group—family, clan, work-group, department, business, industry, country— over that of the individual. It is often expected that an individual will accept harm such as a demotion, pay cut, fine, or other loss of face in order to preserve the face or otherwise reduce harm to a group of which the individual is a member. (It is also thought that this is importantly related to the Chinese religious-philosophical-cultural emphasis on harmony, discussed previously.)

When sociologists like Geert Hofstede and others measure the collectivism-individualism spectrum globally, they find that China leans significantly more towards collectivism than the United States, or Northern and Western Europe (Hofstede, Hofstede, & Minkov, 2010, pp. 90–92). The latter are the most individualist societies, whereas China and Asia generally are among the most collectivist (Hofstede et al., 2010, pp. 92–102). Another interesting finding, which Hofstede and others confirm in their research, is that globally, more people live in societies that tend towards collectivism. This is grist for our mill that Western, but in this case especially American as well as Western and Northern European businesspeople in particular, have very good reason in the global business environment to expand the range of their cultural-ethical-philosophical understanding and fluency. While Europe and North America are economically extremely important parts of the world, to simply assume Western standards are global standards, as many do, is not only naïve but demonstrably inaccurate. These cultural differences help explain the apparent intractability of the challenges that motivated us to write this book. Difficulties communicating and working across this spectrum from more collectivist to more individualist are real because the cultures are profoundly different along this spectrum. That said, any businessperson serious about going to China, staying there, and keeping their hands as clean as can be needs to understand, appreciate, and learn to navigate these differences. On the bright side, since collectivism is more of the global norm than individualism even into the 21st century, this is an investment worth making. Even if, going forward, there comes a global shift towards individualism, there is little to be lost by Western businesses and businesspeople who gain the Agility to work within more collectivist contexts in the meantime.

As is usual in comparing and contrasting differing perspectives on ethics, there is nuance to the individualist-collectivist distinction. Even within Chinese culture and philosophy, collectivism—the generic view that any individual's rights, privileges, interests, and ethical choices are subordinate to the group's—takes a number of forms, as does its inverse, individualism, the more primary value in much of the global Northwest (Wong, 2020). It is precisely this kind of nuance that motivates this book, with its emphasis on the philosophical foundations of culture, in addition to psychological and sociological differences East-to-West. We leave detailed discussions of such nuances to philosophy, psychology, and sociology seminars. What is important for present purposes is that the collective's interests do not simply and totally override individual interests. One can disobey a superior, and even act in a way contrary to what the larger group, company, or even society demands, if one does it in ways consistent with principles such as hierarchy (xiào), propriety (lǐ), and uprightness (yì) discussed in the previous sections. One must be sure that when one acts in any such way, one respects the face of the group and any superiors involved as much as possible. Another complexity is that the further up the hierarchy one goes, both in business and government, the less collectivist the thinking. Xi Jinping, Jack Ma, and Terry Gou, for example, care a very great deal about the prestige and well-being of the collectives they lead, but their behavior is not overtly collectivist, in contrast with middle-managers and even many top executives. This is another matter one must understand about Chinese culture contexts.

A classic illustration of how properly to disobey a superior according to Chinese ethics and culture comes from the Mengzi, in which a cultivated man wishes to marry a woman of whom his parents do not approve (Mengzi, 2008, p. 118). He knows she and he are a perfect match, but the parents do not see it that way and withhold their consent. In this case, there is an apparent conflict between uprightness on the one hand—standing up for what you know to be right, despite inconvenience to yourself as a result of a superior's or society's disapproval—and hierarchy and propriety on the other hand—which require that one respects the wishes and commands of a superior, in this case a parent. The cultivated person in this case marries without their parents' consent so that the parents' face is respected at the same time as the couple is able to wed. The same reasoning would apply in the workplace if a subordinate had to disobey an unethical or problematic order from a superior. The right thing to do is to disobey, but in a way that does not directly or openly challenge the superior, thereby avoiding open conflict. The subordinate should anticipate criticism from the superior (as part of them maintaining their face), and perhaps also some erosion of their relationship with the superior. This only works well, of course, if both parties understand these ethical-cultural norms well enough to accurately anticipate both the actions of the superior and the subordinate. An application of this is a common and much bemoaned problem in China–West business relations—when unaware Westerners find out that Chinese partners or their subordinates have said they would do one thing but instead have done another. Chinese partners or subordinates may think they are disobeying in such a way as to respect the face of their superiors and/or partners, but without understanding on both sides, the situation devolves into blaming and finger-pointing such as we saw in our discussion of the drug supply-chain challenges in Chapter 3.

We should not leave the subject of collectivism without making note of the fact that, together with the emphasis on harmony, the current regime, the Chinese Communist Party, often invokes these values to justify all-encompassing state control of information, including personal information that can be used to identify and repress political dissent. Efforts towards political repression and social control have increased under Xi Jinping, and so it should not be surprising, as we noted in Chapter 1, that Xi has embraced traditional Chinese ethics to justify a very modern, high-tech form of authoritarianism. His embrace of traditional ethics should be viewed as a sign of the enduring power of these traditional values rather than any sort of independent verification of whether the current regime is actually in accordance with them. This question, interesting and important as it is, lay regrettably beyond the scope of this book to adequately analyze and answer, although, for the record, despite their protestations to the contrary, we don't believe Xi or the CCP generally are paragons of traditional Chinese values.

5.4 Parting paradoxes: ethical continuity and change in contemporary China

Earlier in this chapter we noted how traditional Chinese culture is more accepting of paradox than many Western ones, and we have certainly tested that contention with our readers. In the beginning of this book, we acknowledged that traditional Chinese culture was but a part of the current moral climate. Traditional Chinese culture bumps up against pop culture, art, video games, the internet, and contemporary political discourses, to name but a few alternative sources. Moreover, just as there is no denying that traditional Chinese values persist in the modern era, it is abundantly clear that the economic reforms that began over four decades ago have ushered in new ideas about globalization, free market economics, and human rights. How much and in what ways China has changed and what the future will bring continues to be a topic of speculation and debate among China experts. Though it might seem paradoxical and contradictory to some, the authors believe China will change dramatically in the coming decades but that tradition will also endure. The rule of law, human rights, and other Western ideas will inevitably achieve some greater resonance in China in the coming decades. Even so, the traditional Chinese values that have endured over two millennia are very likely to endure as well in some form and strength, and may well influence cultures beyond China's borders. Hence, the authors have no worries that this book will become obsolete anytime soon.

Another paradox that has been a recurrent theme of this book is the idea of ethical fluency, i.e., that one can understand and act within one ethical system while maintaining the core values of another. We have put our theory of ethical fluency into action in case studies involving intellectual property, quality and safety in the drug supply chain, and, in the hardest test, human rights. (Whether our solution represents a Western proclivity to resolve a paradox or a harmonious Chinese embrace of paradox we leave for the reader to decide.) We have been working under the broad idea that two different systems of ethics can address the same concerns about humanity and social/political order, but from differing metaphysical, epistemological, or religious presuppositions. We have shown how traditional Chinese culture offers a fully formed way of looking at the world, and particularly at ethics. For example, if you truly treat people benevolently, then any need for them to assert their human rights is far less acute because you're already treating them well and justly.

This book has attempted to demonstrate that engaging with Chinese perspectives on ethical thought and behavior does not amount to a relativistic "going native," or as the old adage goes, "when in Rome, do as the Romans do." We have shown how ethical fluency can help accomplish precisely the opposite result, i.e., promote preexisting ethical and business objectives more effectively by practicing ethical flexibility or, as we call it, Agility. To elucidate why flexibility in ethics—Agility—does not entail giving up on preexisting ethical principles and values, we return to our metaphor of water, which is central to the classic texts *The Art of War* and the *Daodejing*, and famously invoked by Bruce Lee. Just because water changes its shape to fit whatever container you put it in does not mean that water has no essence of its own. Water has specific chemical properties that cause it to dissolve salt but not oil, that explain surface tension, and so on. Water can exert great power suddenly, as in floods or tsunamis, but it can also slowly wear away hard materials like metal and stone over time. Water adapts its shape yet it still has an inherent nature.

In conclusion, we recall a story told about a Westerner's first trip into China. After US President Richard Nixon's momentous visit to China in 1972, the country slowly opened to the West with fits and starts, most notably in the wake of the 1989 Tiananmen Square massacre. In those first decades of opening to the West, it was not possible to fly into China. The entrepôt city of Hong Kong, then still under British rule, was the entry point into "the mainland." In Hong Kong at that time there was a story told at the famed Foreign Correspondent's Club of a Western journalist making their first trip into China, usually into Guangzhou, which could be reached by a short train trip. (Shanghai at the time was a two-night journey by train from Guangzhou.) The story went that after the first day in China, the wide-eyed Western newbie would exclaim "this place is so interesting. I want to write a book about it." A week later, a bit chastened by all they observed and experienced, they would cut down their expectations and say "perhaps an article will do." After a month, the hope was reduced to the daunting prospect of uttering one sentence about China that did not seem ignorant and foolish.

The authors hope that as the reader comes to the end of this book they will not wish we had confined ourselves to working out that one sentence. We end our book with this story because it perfectly captures two aspects of Western experiences in China. The first is the exhilaration of arriving in such a unique and fascinating place. The second is how in many ways China seems so complicated and difficult for Westerners to understand. This book has attempted to make China a little less complicated for business executives and others, but we hope in doing so that we rekindle in the reader that surge of excitement that they felt on their first trip to China. While we wrote this book as a primer to communicate and operate more effectively in China, we hope that our discussion will also yield some intrinsic personal fulfillment for the reader. We hope it will provide a vehicle for Westerners to experience Chinese culture on a more intimate level, deepen friendships with their Chinese counterparts, and help realize the hope of nearly every Westerner visitor to understand and appreciate this rich and ancient culture.

References

Ames, R. T., & Rosemont, H. (1999). *The analects of Confucius: A philosophical translation.* New York: Ballantine Books.

Angle, S., & Slote, M. (2013). *Virtue ethics and Confucianism.* New York: Routledge.

Associated Press. (2001, March 8). *China decides homosexuality no longer mental illness*. Retrieved from www.hartford-hwp.com/archives/55/325.html

Banister, J. (1992). A brief history of China's population. In D. Poston & D. Yaukey (Eds.), *The population of modern China*. Boston, MA: Springer.

BBC. (2010, January 11). China faces growing gender imbalance. *BBC News*. Retrieved from http://news.bbc.co.uk/2/hi/asia-pacific/8451289.stm

Bian, J. (2019). *Guanxi: How China works*. Medford, MA: Polity Press.

Champion, T., & Aubin, H. (2020, February 4). History of Europe. *Encyclopaedia Britannica*. Retrieved August 13, 2020, from www.britannica.com/topic/history-of-Europe

Chinn, M. (2020, August 17). Personal email communication.

Collinsworth, E. (2014). *I stand corrected*. New York: Doubleday.

Cowen, T. (2011, June 11). "It is too soon to tell"—the real story China fact of the day. *Marginal Revolution*. Retrieved from https://marginalrevolution.com/marginalrevolution/2011/06/it-is-too-soon-to-tell-the-real-story.html

De Menthe, B. L. (2013). *The Chinese way in business*. North Clarendon, VT: Tuttle.

Flannery, R. (2013, April). Solitary woman: Chinese startup culture is a male-dominated world. *Forbes*. Retrieved from www.forbes.com/sites/russellflannery/2013/04/04/solitary-woman/#6838950028fe

Grant, B. (2008). Women, gender and religion in premondern China: A brief introduction. *Nan Nü*, 2–21.

Hall, D., & Ames, R. (1987). *Thinking through Confucius*. Albany: SUNY Press.

Hofstede, G., Hofstede, G. J., & Minkov, M. (2010). *Cultures and organizations: Software of the mind*. New York: McGraw Hill.

Ivanhoe, P. J. (2020, March 9). Author Interview.

Ivanhoe, P. J., & Van Norden, B. W. (2005). *Readings in classical Chinese philosophy* (2nd ed.). Indianapolis: Hackett.

Koh, E. (2008). Gender issues and Confucian scriptures: Is Confucianism incompatible with gender equality in South Korea? *Bulletin of the School of Oriental and African Studies, University of London*, 345–362.

Kroll, P. W. (2017). *A student's dictionary of classical and medieval Chinese* (Revised ed.). Leiden: Brill.

Kung, H., Von Stietencron, H., & Van Ess, J. (1993). *Christianity and world religions*. Maryknoll, NY: Orbis Books.

Liu, Q. (1994). A comparative study and causal analysis of women's family status in contemporary China. *Chinese Journal of Population Science*, 101–111.

Mengzi. (2008). *Mengzi* (B. W. Van Norden, Trans.). New York: Hackett.

Nylan, M., & Wilson, T. (2010). *Lives of Confucius: Civilization's greatest sage through the ages.* New York: Random House.

O'Sullivan, K. (2012, August 10). The role of women in China. *Fair Observer.* Retrieved August 9, 2020, from www.fairobserver.com/region/central_ south_asia/role-women-china/

Paine, L. S. (2002). *Value shift.* New York: McGraw Hill.

Paulson, H. (2015). *Dealing with China.* New York: Hachette.

Reuters. (2015, January 21). China says its gender imbalance "most serious" in the world. *Scientific American.* Retrieved from www.scientificamerican. com/article/china-says-its-gender-imbalance-most-serious-in-the-world/

Rofel, L. (2007). *Desiring China: Experiments in neoliberalism, sexuality, and public culture.* Durham: Duke University Press.

Rozman, G. (Ed.). (1991). *The East Asian region: Confucianism and its modern adaptation.* Princeton: Princeton University Press.

Russell, J. C. (1972). Population in Europe. In C. M. Cipolla (Ed.), *The middle ages: The Fontana economic history of Europe* (pp. 25–71). London: Collins, Fontana.

Sheehan, M. (2017a, June 11). Alibaba helps Chinese LGBTQ couples say "we do" in West Hollywood. *Huffington Post.* Retrieved August 9, 2020, from www. huffpost.com/entry/alibaba-lgbt-couples-west-hollywood_n_7560956

Sheehan, M. (2017b, June 30). Many Chinese cheer for U.S. marriage equality, but what would Confucius say? *Huffington Post.* Retrieved August 9, 2020, from www.huffpost.com/entry/china-gay-marriage-confucius_ n_7701084?guccounter=1&guce_referrer=aHRocHM6Ly9kdWNrZHVVj a2dvLmNvbS8&guce_referrer_sig=AQAAAMcImTowFifinEqUnVbF9I_ cC9BXasFbIzfku67oooughHhLefiTCh3d77AmZZ_TpwsUYx4zjUZC9_cZ_ eiR841snlMs9bWWUo95ASeJh

Shun, K. L. (2002). *Ren and Li in the analects* (B. W. Norden, Ed.). New York: Oxford University Press.

Sunzi. (2011). *The art of war* (P. J. Ivanhoe, Trans.). Indianapolis: Hackett.

Swann, N. L. (1994). Pan Chao: The foremost woman scholar of China. In A. Andrea & J. Overfield (Eds.), *The human record: Sources of global history* (pp. 148–153). Boston: Houghton Mifflin.

Tsoi-lai, C. W. (2015, June 29). US gay marriage ruling sparks debate in China. *Global Times.* Retrieved August 9, 2020, from www.globaltimes.cn/ content/929367.shtml

US Census Bureau. (2020). US and world population clock. Retrieved December 6, 2020, from https://www.census.gov/popclock/world

Van Norden, B. W. (2007). *Virtue ethics and consequentialism in early Chinese philosophy*. New York: Cambridge University Press.

Van Norden, B. W. (2015, July 13). Confucius on gay marriage: The U.S. Supreme Court invokes the Chinese philosopher, with decidedly mixed results. *The Diplomat*. Retrieved August 9, 2020, from https://thediplomat.com/2015/07/confucius-on-gay-marriage/

Verstappen, S. (2015). *Chinese business etiquette*. Berkeley: Stone Bridge Press.

Wenzhong, H., Grove, C., & Euping, Z. (2010). *Encountering the Chinese: A modern country, an ancient culture* (3rd ed.). Boston: Intercultural Press.

Wong, D. (2020, June). Chinese ethics. In E. N. Zalta (Ed.), *The Stanford encyclopedia of philosophy*. Stanford: Stanford University Press.

Xie, Z. (1994, December 11). Regarding men as superior to women: Impacts of Confucianism on family norms in China. *National Library of Medicine*. Retrieved from https://pubmed.ncbi.nlm.nih.gov/12290499/

Xunzi. (1999). *Xunzi* (Vol. 1, J. Knoblock, Trans.). Changsha: Hunan People's Publishing House.

Yang, S. (2016). *Women in transition: Ban Zhao and gender issues*. Retrieved from http://gateway.proquest.com.libproxy.scu.edu/openurl?url-ver=Z39.88-2004&res-dat=xri:pqdiss&rft-val-fmt=info:ofi/fmt:kev:mtx:dissertation&rft-dat=xri:pqdiss:3743739

Yu, K. P., Tao, J., & Ivanhoe, P. J. (2009). *Taking Confucian ethics seriously*. Albany: SUNY Press.

Zhao, B. (1900). *Instruction for Chinese women and girls*. New York: Eaton & Mains.

Zhuangzi, B. (2009). *Zhuangzi: The essential writings: With select . . . (paperback)* (B. Ziporyn, Trans.). New York: Hackett.

方旭东. (2015, June 28). 儒家再发声: 同性婚姻不符合传统儒家对婚姻的理解. *The Paper*. Retrieved August 9, 2020, from www.thepaper.cn/news Detail_forward_1346237

INDEX

Note: Page locators in *italics* represent a figure on the corresponding page.